BILL "READY" CASH & AL HUNTER JR.

THOU SHALT NOT STEAL

The Baseball Life and Times of a Rifle-Armed Negro League Catcher

To Bruce:
Thanks for
keeping Negro League
History alive. Bill's
story is a story about
struggle, survival and
success.

Al Hunter Jr   2/31/12

Cover portrait of Bill "Ready" Cash by photographer Michael Bryant.

Cover photo of Bill "Ready" Cash, Philadelphia Stars catcher from 1943
to 1950, from the John W. Mosley Photographic Collection, Charles L.
Blockson Afro-American Collection, Temple University Libraries.

ISBN-10: 0615445462
EAN-13: 9780615445465
Library of Congress Control Number: 2011921970
Love Eagle Books, Philadelphia, PA

CONTENTS

1. Call Me Bill "Ready" Cash   5

2. The Arrival   9

3. Ready to Play and Work   23

4. Finding Love   31

5. Seeing Stars   35

6. My Fields of Dreams and MVPs   55

7. Trying to Adjust   63

8. Breaking Down the Door   85

9. A Lukewarm Welcome and Red-Hot Lie   107

10. Staying on the Diamond   139

11. Sliding Home   161

12. Oh, and Another Thing…   181

13. Epilogue   199

CHAPTER 1

CALL ME BILL "READY" CASH

✻ ✻ ✻

Most events recorded in history are more remarkable than important, like eclipses of the sun and moon, by which all are attracted, but whose effects no one takes the trouble to calculate.

—Henry David Thoreau

Man, I don't know what got into Larry Doby's head, but he was hauling around third base like nobody's business—head down, dirt flying behind him.

I remember it like it was yesterday. Ruppert Stadium, Newark, New Jersey. May 5, 1946. Opening day for the Negro Leagues. Bottom of the sixth. Two outs. The Philadelphia Stars, my team, was in a tough one against the Newark Eagles, down one to nothing, and getting screwed by the umps. The Eagles' eight thousand fans were excited as all get out.

And here's Larry Doby, one of the best ever to play baseball, trying to score from second on a slow ground out. I mean, what was he thinking? Most players with good sense would've held at third. But Doby wasn't *most* players. The only thing standing between him and home plate glory was little old me, Bill "Ready" Cash.

I whipped off my catcher's mask, snagged the relay throw from first baseman "Doc" Dennis, and went up the third base line. Doby, chugging like a freight train, dove and hit the dirt on all fours, sliding head first for the plate. I hit the dirt on all fours too. And made the tag.

Home plate was four feet behind me.

"Safe!" the umpire screamed.

"Whaaaatt?!" I yelled. Oh, I was mad, I tell you. And when I shot my arms up in the air in protest, my gloved hand smacked the umpire, who was white, under his chin, knocking him to the ground.

Things got crazy after that.

The play nearly caused a riot right there on the field. My teammates came from everywhere to lay the umpire out. One of them kicked him in the butt while he was still on the ground. Fans jumped out of the stands and onto the field. Cops were called to restore order. It took thirty minutes for the dust to settle. And I got kicked out of the game.

The call was bad, just plain bad. A photograph of the play taken by the *New York Amsterdam News* backed me up, but that didn't make no difference to the league office. I got fined twenty-five dollars and suspended for three games.

And to this day, some people think the reason I didn't make it to the majors was because I smacked a white umpire. Shoot, as bad as that call was, I should've stomped him.

Look, I'm not a household name, OK? Josh Gibson, Satchel Paige, Buck O'Neil, Jackie Robinson, Roy Campanella, Monte Irvin—most of these guys were Negro League ballplayers. But there were lots of Negro

League ballplayers like me, excellent athletes who didn't have Josh's power—man, could he crush a baseball—but who were the league's backbone.

We didn't get fame or notoriety like Josh, Satchel, and them, but we were important. In black neighborhoods desperate for hope, we were heroes.

I'm ninety-one now and don't move as fast as I used to. But in my prime? Shoot, I was six-feet one-and-one-half inches, weighed 195 pounds, and could fire a ball to second base faster than a bullet from a .30-30 hunting rifle. Well, at least that's what some guys said—and I'm not going to argue to that.

I spent seventeen years playing semi-pro ball, seven in the Negro Leagues, and I've got the injuries to prove it. Check out the fingers on my right hand. They're all crooked from getting smacked by foul balls and nicked by bad pitches. I've broke two fingers, a thumb, and a leg.

Like I said, I played some ball.

I was picked to play in the famous East-West game—that's what we called the Negro League all-star games—back in '48 and '49. I played in six countries, set records in a couple of leagues, threw out hundreds of base runners, including the legendary "Cool Papa" Bell. I might not have been flashy, but I sure was steady. I was always ready to play ball.

So you're probably wondering if I was so good, why didn't I make it to the majors? Well, the way I look at it, I was a black man with a lot of pride, a lot of talent, but little patience for liars. More on that later.

My family was among the tens of thousands of blacks that left the South in the early 1900s for the promise of jobs up north. I watched America stumble, recover, and grow into the strongest nation in the world. But you know something? I got more respect in countries like Cuba and Mexico than in my own.

I've seen and done a lot in my time on God's green earth. And I thank Him for this chance to share my experiences. Pull up a chair and get comfortable. Man, I do have some stories to tell you.

CHAPTER 2

THE ARRIVAL

* * *

Life consists not in holding good cards but in playing those you hold well.

—Humorist Josh Billings

When Pop saw us get off the train in Philadelphia that day in 1924, he wanted to run and hide. We looked so darn "country."

Pop had been living in Philadelphia for two years and had gotten used to how folks up north dressed—and we didn't even come close. My brothers and I were barefoot, our shoes slung around our shoulders. We weren't used to having shoes on, you know. Back home in rural Round Oak, Georgia, we always went barefoot around the farm because the good Lord took care of us and kept the snakes and other creatures away from our feet. And Mom? Shoot, when we got off that train, she was carrying bedclothes on top of her head like one of those women in Africa. Man, we were a sight!

We'd been riding for days, munching on chicken and biscuits, sipping sodas. My brothers and I had no idea where we were going when we boarded down in Juliette, Georgia. We were just happy to be going *somewhere.* Now we were at the "Chinese Wall" in Philadelphia's old Broad Street Station on May 30, 1924, ready to start a new life up north, glad to see Pop again—and we looked like foreign refugees.

Arthur Cleveland Cash Sr., my father, came to Philadelphia in 1922 to work at the Westinghouse Electric Plant after bollworms ate up our crops back home. Pop was always a hard worker. He saved up his money then sent for us. And after two years in Philadelphia, Pop knew how people up north were supposed to dress. And they always wore shoes. I mean, it shouldn't have been a big surprise to him, though. In those days, Northern blacks fresh from the South expected their Southern relatives to arrive up north looking a little "country," but Pop couldn't believe how "country" we were.

I was five, and my brothers and I didn't care nothing about how we looked; we were just elated to be out of Georgia. We'd be away from the snakes, and my mother, Leila, wouldn't break her back anymore washing clothes in "the branch," a small creek on the farm. In Round Oak, we barely saw Pop because he was always out in our fifty-eight acres, plowing, picking corn, cabbage, and beans. My great-grandfather and great-grandmother helped a little, but mostly it was Mom and Pop who worked the farm. And no matter what, they had to be out there. Mom used to tell me how, just two days after giving birth to her children, she worked right back in the fields, behind the mules, plowing. Man, it was a rough life.

Mom and Pop grew up in Round Oak and met each other as students in the town's one-room schoolhouse. Pop was born out of wedlock to the daughter of Walker Roan and never passed fifth grade—he quit to help Grandpop Walker tend the farm. Mom went as far as sixth or seventh grade, I think. They married in 1912 and stayed with my great-grandpop until moving north.

When I got older, I asked Pop why he left Georgia in 1922. See, I was the only son who sat down with Pop, and I really liked to talk to him about the old times. I thought he might've left the South because maybe he was running from something—maybe my older brother Joe got in a fight with some white boy, and the white boy's family, rather than go after Joe, instead wanted to get my father and string him up—you know, lynch him.

But Pop said, "Nah, it wasn't like that." He said they planted food and crops on that farm—I think we had cotton, corn, cabbage, and some kind of beans—but bollworms always came along and ate them up. That's why he left, and he didn't have no money coming in. Even if they got all their farm vegetables in, he and Mom maybe had five dollars at the end of the year. Like many Southern blacks, Pop heard those grand stories about the North, where a colored man's dream could come true. People down south talked about how the cities up north were full of good-paying jobs for colored folk, nice places to live too. And Pop listened. He knew how bad things were in the South; farms weren't producing much, you had all the lynching, all the segregation.

So Pop, like hundreds of thousands of other colored people in the early 1900s, fled north. They've even given it a name, "The Great Migration." But moving to Philadelphia in 1922 wasn't Pop's first trip north. He said he brought the family up to Detroit in 1917, back when the automobile plants were hiring. Henry Ford, Ransom Olds, and brothers John and Horace Dodge had that city jumping, producing cars like crazy. And during World War I, Detroit needed workers, because the number of European immigrants who normally would've worked in those factories was reduced thanks to the war; plus, there were organized labor strikes. So they asked unemployed coloreds and whites to work inside the factories, and Pop answered the call.

But my family couldn't stay in Detroit because Mom got pneumonia somehow and the doc said she had to get back to Georgia's warm climate or she'd die. So the family returned to the farm where I, William Walker Cash, was born on February 21, 1919, joining my oldest brother, Joseph Benjamin, and next oldest, Arthur Jr. My youngest brother, George "Tip" Thomas, was born later.

I got to tell you, we may not have made any money, but we kids had fun on that farm. I remember we'd take barrel slats, sit on them like a sled, and zoom on down the hill into the creek. We didn't know how dangerous that was, with all those snakes around and stuff. And chores? We didn't know what chores were. Shoot, we were just kids, you know, so everything seemed like fun. What we called chores was helping Mom out, like when she went to wash clothes down in the branch. I remember one time I was with her when she started washing, then she jumped out of the water.

"Get your great-grandpop and tell him to bring his gun," she yelled at me. See, Mom had seen this huge snake in a hole near where she was washing, and yeah, she was a country girl and was used to seeing things like that, but she wasn't taking no chances. Great-grandpop came down with his shotgun and shot the snake. Come to find out when he shot that big snake, there were four or five other little snakes in that hole. He killed them too.

As far as I know, the farm was ours outright, and my great-grandfather had the papers to prove it. We weren't doing no sharecropping or working the land for some white man. But owning land didn't make it grow crops no better, which, like I said, was why Pop left to go north.

We had a close extended family. When my mother's brother, Uncle Obie, got a job at the Westinghouse Electric Co. plant in Lester, Pennsylvania, just outside Philadelphia, he asked his boss if there was room for three more good, hard-working colored men like himself. The boss said yeah, so Pop and the two brothers-in-law, Joseph H. "Jobie" Lloyd and William Day, moved to Philadelphia in '22 and got jobs at the plant.

When we joined Pop in '24, we stayed with my mother's sister, Aunt Pearl, and her husband, William Day, at 7918 Brewster Avenue in Elmwood, where Pop had been living. Elmwood was a two-mile-square area in the city's southwest side, near the airport. It was also called "the Meadows," and after you saw all the fields and farmland in it, you knew why. But it had a residential and business area too, with houses, restaurants, barbershops, and movie theaters.

Let me tell you, back then Elmwood was a really mixed neighborhood—Jews, Swedes, Lithuanians, Italians, Germans, Poles, gypsies, a few Asians, and us coloreds lived there, and we all got along just fine. The great jazz saxophonist Stan Getz and his family lived there too, but I didn't know him. And singer Patti LaBelle was born there in 1944. Elmwood was a nice place to grow up in, and in the '20s, jobs seemed plentiful—many Elmwood folk worked in the nearby plants, like the Baldwin Locomotive Co., Sun Shipbuilding and Dry Dock Co., General Electric Co., and Westinghouse.

Now Aunt Pearl's house was big and all, but after we Cashes moved in, it got small real fast and Pop wanted to get us our own place. Two years later, when a house at 7906 Brewster became available for rent, we moved on down there for ten dollars a month, and my brothers and I paid the rent by getting up at five in the morning to deliver a Jewish newspaper, which paid $7.50 every two weeks. And Mom earned $1.25 a day, plus carfare, working as a domestic for white families.

So we did OK for a while, but a couple of years later, the Depression hit hard and Pop got laid off from Westinghouse. We did what we could to survive, like pick elderberries for ten cents a quart. Now the kids liked the berries in homemade pies, but the grown-ups used them to make some awfully powerful wine. Pop saved money by cooking us white potatoes and spare ribs for dinner, and that's what we ate all week, white potatoes and spare ribs. Yeah, it was cheap. White potatoes you got five pounds for a quarter; spare ribs, five pounds for a quarter. And Pop wasn't a gourmet chef—he burned up a bunch of pots cooking that stuff. Those meals got boring, but we didn't complain because those white potatoes and spare ribs kept us going.

In the summer, I wore winter boots because they were the only shoes we could afford. To keep warm in winter, we'd sometimes go down to the railroad tracks at Seventy-ninth and Eastwick and picked up loose coal that had tumbled from the freight trains heading into the factories. Shucks, some days it seemed all of Elmwood was there snatching up some coal. And sometimes we burned old wooden railroad crossties for heat. Pop would take his boys out in the family's "Hoover Buggy." This was a cart he named after President Hoover. It didn't run on gasoline or steam. No sir, *we* were its power. Pop pulled from the front while we four Cash boys pushed from the back. We'd take that buggy out whenever we went down to dig up those crossties—you know, those pieces of wood that the metal rails are spiked on to. The old crossties were left behind after World War I, after Uncle Sam did some salvage work and removed the metal rails. Anyway, we'd load the ties into the cart, take them home, cut them up with a two-man saw, and burn them at night.

If we wanted to go see a movie at the Crescent Theater at Eighty-fourth and Eastwick, we'd first go to the trash dump and dig for pieces of copper. Then we'd take the metal to the junk shop and trade it in for a few nickels. With those coins jangling in our pockets, we'd run down to the theater and use them to pay our way in. Man, I loved watching those *Flash Gordon* and *Tarzan* movies. And we could sit right next to our white friends and cheer together for our on-screen heroes. Unlike other city theaters, the Crescent wasn't segregated.

To me, there were only two bad things about Elmwood in those days: The mosquitoes—man, they were big—and no sewers. Most homes had outhouses and sometimes people collected the manure and used it for fertilizer. And you know something? That fertilizer made the cabbages grow as big as basketballs.

Yeah, that's how it was living in Elmwood back then. We were poor, but the family stayed strong and together— thanks to Grandmom Mary, my mother's mother, who lived with Uncle Joe. I remember Grandmom Mary ate dinner with us every Friday. And Grandmom Mary's word was it. It didn't matter whether you were grown, married, or whatever. If Grandmom Mary said "shut up," you shut up. Period.

That's not to say we didn't have discipline at home. When we acted up, Pop had a ready answer: that long strap of his. Nowadays, so-called experts say you shouldn't hit your kid if he or she is bad. Shoot, Pop wore our butts out, thank goodness. And at report card time, the first thing Pop looked at was our attendance record. He wanted to make sure we were going to school and not goofing off somewhere. You know, they've taken the Bible and prayer out of our schools, and you can't hit the kids no more. No wonder we're having so many problems with young folk.

Yes sir, Pop was strict (and I admit I picked up some of that in raising my own kids later on). Pop hated craps and didn't want his boys messing with it. He said the game always wound up in one of three ways: an argument, knife cutting, or death.

Tell you how serious Pop was, one day my brothers and I were hanging out on the corner—shooting craps. Don't ask me why. You know how hardheaded kids can be, tell them not to do something and they do it anyway. So we were there playing craps for match covers. And Pop had just come home from work, and Miss Jackson, the neighborhood gossip, couldn't wait to call him and tell him what we were doing.

Pop stormed out of the house, saw my brothers shaking the dice, and headed toward us. I stopped him halfway and started tattling. I was mad at my brothers because we had a fight earlier, so I figured I'd get back at them. "Daddy, Daddy. They're out there playing cards!"

Now Pop had seen them playing craps but didn't say anything. To him, there was a big difference between cards and craps. So that night, just as we were about to go to bed, Pop came into our bedroom with his trusty strap. He wanted to see if we would tell the truth about what we'd been doing that day. If we were honest, he told Mom, nobody's butt would get warm.

He talked to us a little, you know, small talk. Then he asked Tip, "What were you all doing on the corner today?"

Tip pulled the covers up to his face, scared as I don't know what. "We were playing cards," he said.

"So why were you shaking your hands like this?" Pop asked, simulating the craps shooter's motion.

"Shooting..."

Before Tip could say "craps," the covers just flew and Pop was all over him. Then Pop laid into Joe and beat him real good. Then it was Arthur's turn. Then mine. Then he went back to Tip. Shoot, I never forgot that whipping. To top it off, Pop lectured us. "That's a lot of degradation," he said. "A lot of kids done got killed shooting craps." Tell you how strict Pop was about this, when I was a young man playing semi-pro ball, he refused to let me visit the home of our ace pitcher because he had seen him, his father, and another dude playing craps on the street corner.

So for the rest of my life, anytime I saw a craps game, I walked the other way. When I was courting Sadie and rode the subway to North Philadelphia, there was always a big craps game on a street corner near the Susquehanna-Dauphin station. You think I got anywhere near that game? Shoot, I always crossed the street. I didn't want no part of any "degradation."

Now unlike Pop, Mom was a happy-go-lucky woman, a beautiful person who worked hard cleaning and scrubbing floors. Every morning she made biscuits, and our house was filled with the aroma of freshly baked bread.

I figure I got interested in sports around the late 1920s or early 1930s. Baseball was the big sport in those days, and since we had a large extended family in the neighborhood—twelve Lloyd boys and four Cashes— we'd pick a team from among us and challenge the white boys and usually beat them. We didn't have what you could call real baseball equipment. When the big league teams came through to play games in the neighborhood, if they broke a bat, we'd ask them to give us that bat. Very seldom did we have anything like a real ball. And if we got one, we'd tape it up, and that ball would last nine innings or more. You didn't throw it away because it got dirty or anything like that. Finding a place to play was the easy part. Elmwood had lots of farmland, but sometimes we had to use a scythe to cut the high weeds and bring shovels to clear away cow manure in the field.

It was also around this time that I started building my rifle arm. I was around eleven or twelve. Next to our house was a yard, and Arthur and I would go in there, put a piece of wood or a tin can lid on the ground for home plate, and see who could throw strikes. I'd catch for him; he'd catch for me. That's how my arm got so strong—throwing at small pieces of wood and can lids.

Back then, Arthur was the catcher for our family team, and I was the first baseman. But one day, a foul ball smashed Arthur in his face. He threw down his glove and bawled like a baby. "I ain't catching no more," he whined. Shoot, after seeing what happened to poor

Arthur, nobody else wanted to catch. Except me. And I liked it.

As I matured, I realized the catcher, not the coach, runs the team. I remember some games left me with a powerful ache in the back of my head that came from thinking so much—thinking about what pitch to call for, thinking about what the batter did the last time up, thinking about all kinds of stuff.

But there was more than sports going on in my young life. Adjusting to life up north wasn't hard. I didn't get teased or nothing like that; no one called me a "country bumpkin" or anything. And I got used to wearing shoes. I was enrolled in McKean Elementary School at Eighty-second Street and Tinicum Avenue, but it was overcrowded, so in 1928, the city built Wolf School at Eighty-second Street and Lyons Avenue. I got transferred there, and that's when trouble started. I fought nearly every day. And you'd think it was because someone called me a name or didn't like the way I dressed. Nope. I was getting in fights because I was winning at marbles all the time. Marbles! I'd win and they'd run me home. I stayed at Wolf one semester before going back to McKean.

The first time I caught a "real" baseball game must've been around 1935, and I was about sixteen. And from then on, every time I put on a baseball uniform, no matter what, I was ready to play. That's why I got nicknamed "Ready." From the start, I was a serious, no-nonsense ballplayer. I was on our little neighborhood team—I don't even know if it had a name. We were scruffy, with mismatched uniforms and third-hand baseball bats. One Sunday, the big team in our neighborhood, the Elmwood Grays, was scheduled to play, but their opponent didn't show. And the Grays needed to play to get paid. So our "booking agent," Rob Williams, who was also our second baseman, arranged for us to play the Grays—right after we played two other five-inning games.

After those games, which we won 5-1 and 5-0, we got on a flatbed truck and rode to Eighty-second Street and Lyons Avenue to play the Grays. I was the second-string catcher, and Pop didn't want me playing against the older guys because I was a skinny little thing. "Their game is too fast. You're only a youngster," he said. "You'll get hurt."

Our first-string catcher was Marvin Robinson. Now Marvin was in his twenties and loved to party. He had been out drinking the night before and was half-drunk when he showed up to play that Sunday. He caught the two early games, but by the time the Grays game rolled around, Marvin was sick as a dog. And the hot afternoon sun didn't help. In the third inning, Marvin passed out right there behind home plate.

"Bill, you gotta go in and catch," Rob told me. So I put all the equipment on and settled in behind the plate. First person up was Mack "Motor Mouth" Morrison, the opposing catcher. He smacked a single. His teammates started hollering, "Mack, you gonna steal on that little kid? You gonna steal on that little kid?"

Mack, showing why he got the nickname "Motor Mouth," shouted back, "Yeah, I'm gonna take up a base. I'm gonna take up a base." I heard this and thought, *Not on me, you won't.*

So Mack took off for second. I snagged the pitch, uncoiled, and fired a strike to second base, nailing him. Well, the fans got all over the guy, laughing at him, yelling, "You let that little kid throw you out?!" Motor Mouth's mouth had plumb run out of gas. I just smiled and settled in behind the plate. We beat the Grays 6-2. After that game, I knew catcher was my position. And I was ready to play.

CHAPTER 3

READY TO PLAY AND WORK

* * *

*Train your head and hands to do, your head and heart
to dare.*

—Poet Joseph Seamon Cotter Jr.

Robert Baynard, an old-timer who used to manage the semi-pro Anchor Giants and once managed the Elmwood Grays, was at the "Motor Mouth" game. He liked the way we youngsters played and beat the big boys. He had plans for us. "You kids wanna keep the team going?" he asked.

"Yeah," we said. "We want to keep it going." Shoot, we loved baseball. And this was way before TV, Xbox 360, and hip-hop music became the fun things for kids. So while we had chores and school to worry about, baseball gave us colored kids a way to have fun.

We held team meetings and threw a house party every week in Buck North's big old house—that house must've had a million car tires around it—and raised enough money to get uniforms. The next year we were Elmwood's newest team, the Liberty Stars. We played in a pasture at Seventy-ninth Street and Eastwick Avenue, which during the day was filled with cows. They'd bring them off around 4:30 or 5:00 p.m. because they had to milk them, you know, and we had to go out there with our shovels and shovel the manure off our playing field.

Sometimes we didn't get all of it. I remember one evening, I think it was John Beckham, our left fielder, missed a pile while cleaning around his position. Later he was running for a fly ball and slipped right in one of them and boom! Fell on his butt.

We all laughed at that, but I was becoming more serious about playing and winning. Robert Bembry Jr. was our batboy, and Bob Baynard was his stepfather. To this day, Bob Bembry remembers a game where our pitcher wasn't throwing strikes, and I was getting madder than a hornet. I went out to the mound and took the ball from him. I told him I'd pitch, and he should take my place at catcher. That's what happened, and as it turned out, we won the game with me on the mound. Yeah, I could be a strict, take-charge guy at times, but usually when I was in control, things worked out for the best.

Around this time, I was seventeen and in high school. After leaving Wolf Elementary School, I went to the neighborhood junior high, Tilden, then traveled across the city to Overbrook High. The teams at Overbrook were called the Panthers a.k.a the Hilltoppers. Years after I was gone, a young basketball player named Wilt Chamberlain played at 'Brook and would make the school known around the country. Anyway, I was a good student and liked shop and math classes. Some days after school, I'd go to McKean Elementary to pick up young Bob Bembry and other neighborhood kids and walk them home. Sometimes we played soccer in a field behind the school right across from the firehouse. Once we got home, I helped the kids with their homework.

Bob said even back then I was firm but wasn't a dictator. I guess I've always liked working with kids, even when I was a kid myself.

During my junior year, I was the only black on Overbrook's baseball team, and I was angry as all get out. We had this coach named Mr. Kistenmacher, and he started another catcher, whose name I think was Roseoff or Rubof, over me. Both were Jewish, and like other immigrants, Kistenmacher was probably looking out for his own, but that still didn't make it right. I could out-catch, out-throw, and out-hit Roseoff, but Kistenmacher had me as a second-string shortstop. Now I could play any position, but my heart was in catching, and Kistenmacher knew it, but he was starting this other guy ahead of me, even though I was better than he was.

Looking back, this was my first taste of racism, a taste that grew more bitter as I grew older. Years later, as a respected Negro League catcher, I ran into Mr. Kistenmacher again—and he had the nerve to act like he always knew I was good and that he had helped me get to where I was. But while he grinned and patted himself on the back for my success, I seethed inside, remembering how he promoted a second-rate player over me in high school.

And I never got to finish high school. Like many families, ours was hurt by the Great Depression. When those stocks tumbled in 1929, the impact spread like ripples in our Round Oak stream—factories shut down, banks and stores closed, millions of folks were left jobless. Pop got laid off from Westinghouse in 1929 and stayed out for five years. By the time Franklin D. Roosevelt became president and started trying to fix things, the Depression was four years old. Franklin

Roosevelt's "New Deal" program provided jobs, some help for the poor, and changes to businesses and government to keep such a thing from occurring again. Many jobs came out of the Civilian Conservation Corps (CCC), which started in 1933, and the Work Projects Administration (WPA), which got going in 1935.

Even after Pop got his job back at Westinghouse in 1933, we were still bad off. My brothers were working construction, making twenty-five dollars a week at non-WPA jobs, but weren't contributing money to the household. That bothered me—and I was just a teenager.

I couldn't stand seeing Mom and Pop struggle, so in 1936, just a few months before my graduation, I dropped out of Overbrook and went to work. My first job was busting up old railroad ties for a man we called "Knockie" because he was so knock-kneed. We'd go by the airport, dig up the crossties, split them with sixteen-pound sledgehammers, then sell the wood. He paid me one dollar a day. It wasn't the kind of money my brothers were making, but it was more than we had before.

I left Knockie to work for Mr. Reynolds, who also paid me one dollar a day. He was a nice family man and had some mighty pretty daughters who caught my eye. Plus Mr. Reynolds didn't sell busted-up wood. He was an ice-and-coal man, one of the most important people in our neighborhood. They were so important that Elmwood had three of them. Electricity wasn't widespread back then, so most families depended on the ice-and-coal men to bring ice to refrigerate their food and coal to heat their homes.

And let me tell you, this wasn't an easy job. The ice-and-coal man took three hundred-pound blocks of ice from the ice house and, while in the back of his truck, chipped the blocks into smaller chunks with an ice pick. Then he'd stick the chunks in a leather pouch, sling it over his shoulder, and deliver the ice to his customers. Those pouches held one hundred pounds of ice easy. I know, because six days a week I carried ice, sometimes up four flights of steps. It seemed like people on the top floors always wanted the biggest pieces of ice and the most buckets of coal.

After working with Mr. Reynolds six months, I went to work for another ice-and-coal man, Mr. Rogers. He preferred making time with the ladies on his route rather than work, and that bugged me. I didn't have no time for that nonsense, because I wanted to do the job, then go home.

Still, I stayed for nearly two years then went to work for Mr. Jackson, who upped my pay to nine dollars a week.

Now Mr. Jackson didn't believe in socializing like Mr. Rogers, but he couldn't count money to save his life. He struggled to give customers change, slowing down deliveries on the route. It's a wonder how he stayed in business. Once, before I knew he had a money-counting problem, he paid me a dollar too much. I thought he was testing my honesty. "Look, Mr. Jackson. I don't want to take nothing that's not mine," I said. After a while, I convinced him to let me handle the change, and we finished the route quicker.

Hauling ice and swinging sledgehammers made me muscular, and that gave me even more confidence to face my older brothers. You know me, I had to make things right. I had to get things straight with Arthur and Joe. It wasn't fair that Mom had to work hard for those white people, get paid peanuts, then come home and fix us dinner.

So one day I asked them, "Do you guys want hot food when you come home?"

"Yeah, yeah."

"Look," I said, "you're going to give Mom five dollars a week, and I'm going to give her four." That way, Mom wouldn't have to work and she wouldn't be so tired when she had to fix us dinner. Well, they agreed.

I was playing ball with the Liberty Stars, and we had a good team. In 1938, we played seventy-two games and only lost four. There were times we outdrew the big-time Elmwood Grays. People lined up down the railroad tracks and along the pasture to watch us play. And we weren't playing for pay. We just loved the game. And they loved watching us. Baseball was an escape as well as a social affair for the neighborhood. Occasionally, the hat was passed among the spectators, but we never saw the money. I figure it went to Bob Baynard, who kept us in sharp uniforms and supplied us with good baseballs and bats.

We entered the Pennsylvania League with the Wayne Black Hawks, Main Line Tigers, North Philly Raiders, and a team from Oakeola, Pennsylvania, near Sharon Hill. We did well. The only team to give us trouble was Oakeola.

One day during spring training in 1939, I noticed two men watching us during infield practice. One was Robert Smallwood, the other Otto Briggs. Smallwood had been a good sandlot ballplayer. We all knew about Otto "Mirror" Briggs, who had played right field on the great Hilldale team in the Negro Leagues. Smallwood and Briggs were starting a team in Camden, New Jersey, called the Giants and needed a catcher. We had three: Me, Marvin Robinson, and "Radio" Owens. Bob told the men they could take either Marvin or Radio, but they wanted me. After practice, Bob called the team together and said it was breaking up because Briggs and Smallwood wanted me to play in Camden.

"Don't worry, we won't be going anywhere," I said. I planned to stay with the Liberty Stars, because they were my friends.

So I was surprised when I got home and discovered Briggs and Smallwood had already visited Pop. "If they're going to pay you, then you're going to work for them," he said.

That did it. Two days later, I was at Seventeenth and Fitzwater streets, warming up a pitcher for the Camden Giants named Jim Lewis. Afterward, Briggs came over and handed me two dollars. Two dollars! Shoot, that was a lot of money for doing something I enjoyed. And I didn't have to haul no ice or coal to earn it.

Two weeks later, I was nervous as all get out. It was opening day in Camden, and we were playing the barnstorming Baltimore Black Sox. There I was, a kid in the starting lineup, who until a few weeks ago was playing baseball for fun, not for money. Camden had players from the Philadelphia Stars of the Negro National League: Bill Casey was playing third, and Bud Mitchell, a catcher, was on the bench. All of this was whipping through my head when Briggs called me over and sat me down. He knew I had butterflies.

He said, "Cash, whenever any manager feels you're good enough to be in the lineup, consider yourself as good as any ballplayer on the field."

I was never nervous again.

CHAPTER 4

FINDING LOVE

✳ ✳ ✳

*For it was not into my ear you whispered, but into
my heart.*
It was not my lips you kissed, but my soul.
                              —Entertainer Judy Garland

Man, she was the prettiest gal I had ever seen, but
I had to step on her foot to get her attention.
I remember the date exactly: the eighteenth
day of February, nineteen hundred and forty. A few
members of the Counts (a neighborhood club) and I
had been at the Germantown Skating Center when my
cousin Rich Lloyd invited us to a birthday party for a girl
named Sue Norris. We were always looking for a chance
to meet the ladies, so when the rink closed at midnight,
Forest Hill, Curtis Bellows, Rich, and I got into our cars
and drove through the snow-covered streets to the party.

It was still jumping when we arrived. And I went to
work. I tried to meet every girl in the place. I wouldn't
call it flirting, just good public relations.

Anyway, I was dancing with Rich's girlfriend in the
living room and not paying attention to what I was doing
when I stepped on some gal's foot. Well, Sadie Brooks
didn't like that. She was sitting in the chair because
she was tired, and here I come stepping on her toes. I

apologized and just kept dancing. Miffed, she tucked her feet up under her in the chair so I wouldn't make the same mistake twice.

Around 2 a.m., everyone was arranging rides home. I was driving my cousin's coupe. Sue's father, Mr. Norris, asked me to take his girlfriend and this other gal to work. They were domestics and lived in the houses they worked in. Mr. Norris' girlfriend worked in Drexel Hill. The other gal worked in Chestnut Hill.

Now, I thought I had said hello to every good-looking girl at the party. Apparently this one had escaped me. She was wearing a beautiful little hat with flowers.

"Pardon me," I said. "I don't think I met you."

"My name is Sadie Brooks," she said, remembering I stomped her toes.

"I'm Bill Cash," I said. And at that moment, this gal wearing the beautiful little hat with flowers stole my heart.

Since I'm driving a coupe, everyone, including Mr. Norris, had to sit up front. Sadie wound up in Mr. Norris' lap. Whenever I drove by a street lamp, I'd steal a glance at Sadie and watch how the light set her lovely face aglow. Man! When we got to Drexel Hill, Mr. Norris walked his girlfriend to the door. Alone with Sadie, I started talking a blue streak. I kept telling her how good she looked and everything. Did she have a boyfriend? Could I see her tomorrow? She told me to meet her at Sue's house the next day, figuring I was just jiving and wouldn't show up.

Shoot, I was at Sue's house at the appointed time, maybe even a few minutes early. And I waited for two hours before Sadie's worried friend finally called her and told her I was there. It was then that Sadie realized I was serious about her, and Cupid shot that arrow. We got married September 7, 1940 and stayed married sixty-three years. She is the prettiest woman I've ever seen, you hear me? Ever.

Like me, Sadie came from the South. She was raised by her mother, Victoria Clark, and her stepfather in Alamo, Georgia, a town so small it's not even on the map. When she and her older sister, Eva Mae, finished school they were sent to New York City to work as domestics.

There was this white lady in Alamo who found jobs for the young colored girls in town. She had a daughter in New York and suggested the colored girls go north to work for her daughter. So the daughter got her friends black maids from Alamo. This wasn't a bad deal for the Alamo women. There wasn't anything for them to do in that little town. Plus in those days, few colored women went to college.

The first family Sadie worked for in New York was a widow and her son. They had a big place, Sadie said, and the widow treated Sadie like her own child. Sadie couldn't have been more than fifteen. Sadie got to Philadelphia thanks to Eva Mae. A minister headed the family Eva Mae worked for in New York. They moved to Chestnut Hill, a high-class neighborhood in Philadelphia. The minister's next-door neighbor wanted a maid too, so Eva told Sadie, and Sadie got a job with the Pierce family. Sadie thinks Mr. Pierce was a lawyer—he left for work each day with a briefcase. He, his wife, and son were rich and very nice. Sadie didn't have to work hard for them. In fact, Mrs. Pierce helped Sadie cook and clean. During her free time, Mrs. Pierce played tennis. Their house was like a palace, and Sadie said she had the entire third floor to herself. And since there were so many black maids in the neighborhood, they often got together and socialized.

Sadie said she had no interest in men. "They always made me sick, trying to kiss you and carry on," Sadie said. "I just was not man-crazy." Well, if you saw how good-looking Sadie was, you'd understand why so many men were interested in her. But Sadie was tough. "We'd go skating in Germantown and what not, and when a fellow tried to be fresh with me, I'd knock 'im down," Sadie said.

She was seventeen and already on her own. Her good looks caught the eye of many men, including boxer Bob Montgomery, the light heavyweight champion. She claims it was nothing serious, they were just friends. No matter, I got the knock out. I got Sadie.

In 1940, I had no idea my baseball career would become the center of our lives, that we would live in countries like Mexico, Cuba, the Dominican Republic, and Canada, where black folks were treated with more respect than in our very own United States. I had no idea I would go against Negro League players like Josh Gibson or "Cool Papa" Bell.

There was a lot on the horizon for Sadie and me.

And a lot of baseball to be played.

CHAPTER 5

SEEING STARS

* * *

A good catcher is the quarterback, the carburetor, the lead dog, the pulse taker, the traffic cop and sometimes a lot of unprintable things, but no team gets very far without one.
— Miller Huggins, Hall of Fame manager

I was twenty-one in 1940 and knew Uncle Sam might come after me. But I wasn't too concerned about that. All of my attention was on finding work, keeping Sadie happy, and carving out time to play ball on Sundays.

By now, the United States was gearing up for a fight. It OK'd the sale of war materiel to Britain and would start a "peacetime" draft later in the year. It even rationed gasoline, and that made traveling to ball games tough. That's one reason why I left the Camden Giants that year and joined the Bacharach Giants.

The Bacharach Giants was another semi-pro team, but was based in Philadelphia, not New Jersey. I didn't stay with them very long—I think it was about two months—but I remember that day we traveled to Atlantic City to play a team that had John Henry "Pop" Lloyd, the game's greatest shortstop.

Now some folks called "Pop" the "black Honus Wagner," but he didn't need to be compared to no white man to be considered good. Tall and lanky, "Pop" moved like a cat. He'd been playing ball since the 1900s, and by the time I saw him in Atlantic City, he was fifty-six years old but, shoot, he was coaching and playing first base like he was twenty. He'd officially ended his career in 1931 with the New York Black Yankees.

I don't remember the name of the team "Pop" was on that day—it might've been the Johnson Stars or the Farley Stars—and I don't remember the final score. But "Pop" made quite an impression on me; he was a nice, mild-mannered guy who took young ballplayers under his wing. By the way, he got into the baseball Hall of Fame in 1977.

So after I left the Bacharach Giants, I joined the Philadelphia Black Meteors, another semi-pro team. Now you might be wondering why I bounced from team to team like a darn ping-pong ball. I wasn't hard to please; it was just a matter of money. Whatever team paid the most and gave me a chance to play the most, that's where I went. We Negro League players did this all the time and called it "jumping."

Anyway, the Black Meteors' home games were played on weekends at Twenty-sixth Street and Snyder Avenue. Man, that field was a dust bowl. Sometimes Sadie would bring our firstborn, Bill Jr., to watch me play, and before the game, that kid would get on the field, and in two seconds flat, he'd be covered with dirt.

I was working full-time at Westinghouse Electric and playing ball on the weekends. Pulling double-duty like that was exhausting, but not as exhausting as dealing with ignorant, racist co-workers. When I was hired at

Westinghouse, I followed the footsteps of my brothers
and a bunch of Lloyd family members. There were
twenty-one of us Cashes and Lloyds working there. And
two other related families, the Kilabrews and the Stiffs,
had almost the same number. Chick, a factory guard,
used to joke, "You know who runs Westinghouse? The
Cashes, the Lloyds, the Kilabrews, and the Stiffs."

But shoot, in reality, we weren't running nothing
except our mouths. I was a floor sweeper, a degrading
job because not only did I sweep, I cleaned the office
and picked debris and trash from around the machines.
I was a glorified maid. Yeah, it paid $21.65 a week, a
lot of money in the 1940s, but I wanted to do more
than just clean up somebody else's mess. And when I
saw those idle engine lathes just sitting there because
the bosses couldn't find enough "qualified" people—
you know, white boys—to run them, I would get really
ticked.

Only fourteen of the twenty-two engine lathes, which
made spindles for electricity, were used. When I cleaned
around those machines, I'd sneak a peek at the machine
operator's blueprints, which were left lying around. Now,
I knew what I was reading. I started drawing blueprints
back in the seventh grade and was good at engineering
and math, so this wasn't gibberish. I enjoyed it. But if an
operator saw me reading those blueprints, he'd come
running toward me all panicky, shouting, "Don't touch!
Don't touch! Don't touch!" Like I was going to mess
up the blueprints by just looking at them. Hell, I knew
more about them than he did. I never said anything to
them, but I made a decision: I was going to night school
to become a machinist. "Those guys aren't any better
than me," I told Pop. "I can do all that work."

And I was right. I did well in night school, which was held at Overbrook, my old high school. My teacher was Mr. Filippone, and whenever anybody wanted something made in shop class, they came to me. I knew my stuff, theory, tool sharpening, measuring to micrometer size. I tested out second best in the class. The only guy ahead of me was Jordan Oliver, an assistant football coach at Villanova. I got my machinist certificate in January 1943. "Cash," Mr. Filippone told me, "you'll be all right."

But things weren't all right on the job. I had had my fill of Jim Bush, a white foreman who talked to black people like they were animals. He wanted us to be so scared of him we'd do whatever he wanted us to. And I wasn't having it no more.

One morning, my cousin Lou Lloyd, another guy, and I were talking at the plant around 8:45. We all did the same job, but on different shifts, so I had a plan to make the job easier on all of us if we worked together. "Look, if a machine is half dirty, pull it out and clean it out," I said. "That way, the next man won't have nothing to do, just sweep the floor." The fellas liked the idea. We weren't breaking no rules or nothing, just using our heads to make a nasty job more pleasant.

Anyway, we had just finished our little meeting and were about to start sweeping when that cracker Jim Bush comes roaring out of his office, which seemed a block away. Lou's eyes got big as saucers. "Man, we better get," he said. Lou was always running, but this time, I grabbed him and talked to him. "What are you running from? He doesn't even know what we were talking about."

Bush, all out of breath, finally got to us. "Did you see me coming?" he said, sounding all angry and what not.

"Yeah, I saw you coming," I said, cool as one of those ice blocks I used to haul. "You got something for me to do in my shop? Let me know what you want."

Bush didn't like my attitude. See, I was not all scared and intimidated by him like Lou and the other fellas. So he started talking to me like a dog. He said, "Come with me and clean up the chips in the main aisle." Well, first of all, Bush's boss didn't want him messing with us sweepers. And second of all, the main aisle wasn't my responsibility.

So I said, "That's not my job."

Man, that got him hot. "You either go do that job or come down to the office to get your papers," he said, all flustered. He's looking to fire me.

So I went to Mr. Nugent, Bush's boss, and explained what happened. Nugent called Bush in and said to him, "Didn't you hire a man to do that job you want Cash to do?" Well, Bush started to hem and haw because he had hired a man, a friend of mine named Enos Colter, to do that work. But Enos went into the service two weeks earlier, and no one had replaced him.

It didn't matter much. The white guys stuck together. Mr. Nugent pulled me aside and said, "Cash, go clean it up."

Talk about getting angry, man, I was furious. But I didn't act out. I got back at them the best way I could. Instead of doing my job in my normally efficient way, I took my good old time. A job that I breezed through in thirty minutes took me two hours that day. I messed around, talked to the machinists, did all kinds of things to kill time. At exactly 11:30 a.m., the end of my shift, I left the floor, washed, and walked out of Westinghouse to look for a new job.

I was still playing baseball for lots of fun and little money because, to be honest with you, I never thought of becoming a professional ballplayer. I left the Black Meteors and jumped to the Philadelphia Daisies in 1942, and I got some satisfaction when we beat the Meteors four games that year. But World War II still touched our young lives. Since I was married, a skilled laborer, and had an ulcer problem, I escaped the draft. But many healthy unskilled single ballplayers were pulled in to fight for Uncle Sam. Negro League players like first baseman Buck O'Neil, second baseman Larry Doby, and shortstop Monte Irvin spent time doing service for their country. In 1943, one of the players taken in the draft was the catcher for the Philadelphia Stars, and that opened the door for me to join them.

The Stars had been around for eight years. Ed Bolden started them when his powerful Hilldales, an independent team from nearby Darby, Pennsylvania, dissolved after the 1931 season. Ed, a black man, had a history with the Negro Leagues, going back to the 1920s. After a shaky start in 1920–1922, Hilldale became one of the top-flight teams in the early Eastern Colored League, which Ed founded. In fact, Hilldale won the league pennant in 1924, but lost to the Kansas City Monarchs in the first Black World Series.

Ed had a day job at the Thirtieth Street Station Post Office in Philly. With the help of big-time Pittsburgh numbers king William A. "Gus" Greenlee—shoot, that man supposedly took one hundred thousand dollars of his money and built the first black-owned ballpark—Ed worked with a group of black businessmen and women, many of whom were into illicit businesses, and started the new Negro National League in 1933. Along with

Ed were Alex Pompez with the New York Cubans; Abe Manley and his wife, Effa, of the Newark Eagles; Ed Semler of the New York Black Yankees; Tom Wilson of Nashville; and Sonny Jackson of the Homestead Grays.

The Stars were really owned by Eddie Gottlieb, a white businessman who made Bolden a minority owner of the club, but Bolden got most of the ink and was considered by the press the Stars' owner.

The Stars operated as an independent team in 1933. They officially joined the New Negro League in 1934 with Webster McDonald, once one of the best pitchers in the Negro Leagues, as its manager. McDonald developed a reputation for consistently beating the white teams from so-called organized ball. He also managed the Stars to their only Negro League championship in '34.

The 1942 draft swept up many ballplayers, black and white, and dropped them into the service. In 1943, when the Stars' starting catcher—it was either W.T. Cooper or Clarence "Spoony" Palm—went into the army, McDonald didn't have to look far for a replacement.

He'd seen me play with the Philadelphia Daisies in 1942 over at Hilldale Park. He liked my style and asked me to try out for the Stars. I figured, shoot, I had nothing to lose and thought I'd be fighting several other catchers to make the team. The Stars had spring training at their home field at Forty-fourth Street and Parkside Avenue. They also played at Shibe Park, Twenty-first Street and Lehigh Avenue (which years later was renamed Connie Mack Stadium in honor of the great Philadelphia Athletics manager), but only on Monday nights when the A's and Philadelphia Phillies, which shared the stadium, were on the road.

Well, I made the team. And I wish I had a good story to tell you about how tough it was and how I beat three other catchers by throwing out nine base stealers and smacking four homers in a row. Yeah, well, it turned out I didn't have to out-perform anybody. They only brought one catcher in—me. I was elated. I had made it to the Negro Leagues. And I wasn't nervous. Ever since Otto Briggs sat me down in 1939 and said to me "consider yourself as good as any ballplayer on the field," my confidence never flagged.

So in 1943, we opened against the Baltimore Elite Giants. Man, they had a powerful team, with catcher Roy Campanella and a center fielder named Henry Kimbro. Now Kimbro could fly like the wind. So while the Giants took batting practice, we huddled in the dressing room and tried to figure out how to keep Kimbro from stealing.

Our first baseman, Jim "Shifty" West, said to me, "Cash, whenever somebody's gonna steal, we'll yell, 'He left! He left!' That's the signal, OK?" That was good enough for me. So during the game, Kimbro reached first. I was concentrating like crazy, trying to get my pitcher to throw strikes, when suddenly I heard, "He left! He left!" and saw a blur out of the right corner of my eye. I snagged the pitch and unfurled a perfect throw to second that arrived in plenty of time, and Kimbro was out by a mile. That's what got the grapevine talking about me, a youngster with a powerful arm. When the Giants played the Homestead Grays later that week in Richmond, Virginia, the Giants players warned them about me. Kimbro said, "You guys going to Philadelphia to play the Stars? You better watch out, they got a good catcher that can throw."

But when the Grays arrived, they weren't worried about some raw rookie catcher, especially since they had James Thomas "Cool Papa" Bell, the fastest man in baseball. He may have been in the twilight of his career, but the outfielder was still faster than some twenty-year-olds and continued to steal over one hundred bases a year.

Now this is what happened. Cool, batting leadoff, singles. Jerry Benjamin was in the batter's box when I stepped back to check out Cool on first. Before the game, I got a quick scouting report about Cool. If he took a long lead, he wasn't going nowhere. But if he took a short lead, watch out. So I looked at Cool, and he's barely off first.

On the second pitch, West hollered, "He left! He left!" I jumped out of my crouch, shot the ball to second, and by the time Cool started his slide, there's our shortstop waiting for him, ball in glove, and tagged him out.

"I don't believe it. I don't believe it," I heard Cool mutter as he trotted back to the dugout. And you know something? He never tried to steal on me again.

I had a lot to learn and much to get used to in the Negro Leagues, but I was a patient pupil. I had two great teachers on the team, pitchers Barney Brown, our ace left-hander, and right-hander Chet Buchanan. Whenever we played the big teams, like the Monarchs, we always had Barney ready.

He and Chet schooled me on how to get a batter to react to a pitch then throw away from him. I learned that in the Negro Leagues, you pitched to a batter's weakness. In "organized" ball—that's what they called the all-white major leagues back then—the pitchers didn't care about a batter's weakness. If the pitcher had a smoking fastball, that's what he threw and tried to overpower the hitter. The Negro Leagues believed in finesse; they believed in force.

In my first year with the Stars, I hit .323. I was consistent, not flashy at the plate. But it was behind the plate where I was strongest. The Monarchs christened me "30-30," saying my arm was as powerful as a .30-30 rifle. That first year, the Stars had Jim "Shifty" West at first; Mahlon Duckett at second; Gervis "Junior" Fagan at short; Henry "Splo" Spearman at third; Roy "Red" Parnell in left; Homer "Goose" Curry, who doubled as our coach, in right; and Gene Benson in center. It was a good, cohesive team.

"Shifty" got his nickname because he was always shifting around first base. He could make some great plays but had trouble catching a ball with two hands. I remember one game during my rookie year, we had a signal: If a base runner was too far off first, Shifty would take off his glove between pitches, and I'd whip the ball down to first and try to pick him off. So Shifty gave me the signal and I fired that ball to him—and he missed it.

"You had him dead to rights," Goose said to him later in the dugout.

"You know why I missed it?" Shifty said. "I was trying my damnedest to catch it."

When I went to Yankee Stadium in my rookie year and saw where the greatest hitter that ever lived in my book, Josh Gibson, parked some baseballs, I was in awe. Right after we arrived at the stadium to play the New York Black Yankees, one of our pitchers, Henry MacHenry, called me over. "Hey, Cash, I want to show you where Josh hit one on me one-handed," he said.

"See that flag up there on top of the pavilion? That's where he hit it."

Now I'm thinking, wait a minute. From home plate to the base of the outfield fence was about 444 feet. The pavilion was seven stories high. How could a man hit a ball that far? MacHenry must've sensed my doubts, so he called over Spearman, Duckett, West, Benson, and Parnell. "Where did that ball go that Josh hit on me?"

Each one said, "By that flag."

Well, I found first-hand they weren't exaggerating. Griffith Stadium in Washington, D.C., was huge: 405 feet down the left field line, the longest in baseball. It had a twenty-five-foot-high fence and twenty-five rows of bleachers. Behind the bleachers was this big hot-dog sign. Josh hit that hot-dog sign on us four times while I was with the Stars. One year in New Castle, Pennsylvania, Josh crushed—and I mean crushed—a ball so far, it hit the base of the center field fence 505 feet away on one hop.

We seldom got Josh out. Shoot, we were happy if he just hit a single or a double. There was this one game at Forty-fourth and Parkside where Josh hit a line drive so hard it tore the webbing out of shortstop Frank Austin's glove. And by the time Benson tracked down the ball, Josh had circled the bases and was sitting on the bench. Nowadays people are all excited by the long, towering home runs hit by Barry Bonds, Mark McGwire, and Sammy Sosa. But Josh hit balls like that all the time like it was nothing.

Then there was Satchel Paige.

The first time I was supposed to face Satchel, though, I almost quit the team. The Kansas City Monarchs came to Philadelphia in 1943, and when that team came to town, the Negro community buzzed with excitement. Everybody wanted to be at that Monday game in Shibe Park. Satchel Paige and the Monarchs were like Michael Jordan and the Chicago Bulls used to be.

The previous day, sick as a dog, I caught a double-header against the Bushwicks, a club of white major league players who didn't go into the service. Now, the Bushwicks were popular and played a Negro team nearly every weekend, but they didn't play fair. When the Negro teams came to Dexter Parks in Queens, New York, the Bushwicks had two sets of baseballs ready. One was kept cold in a refrigerator or icebox; the other set stayed at normal temperature. When we Negro Leaguers batted, the Bushwicks pitchers used cold baseballs because they don't travel far. When the Bushwicks batted, they used regular balls. The Bushwicks drew more than the Brooklyn Dodgers, and their fans were amazing. They knew all of the Negro League teams and players. They'd greet us by name when we passed through Dexter Park's gates. They made us feel good.

Anyway, in the seventh inning of the first game, I poured ice water over my head to get myself together. I don't know what was wrong with me. So after barely making it through the first game, I went to talk to Goose. I told him I couldn't catch the second game.

Goose didn't care. "Well, I don't have nobody else," he said. He was right: I was the only catcher on the team, and if I got hurt, I don't know what would've happened. So I went to lay down in the dressing room before taking the field for the second game. I doused myself with more ice water in the fifth inning, but I managed to complete the game.

When we returned to Philadelphia that night, I went to my third-shift job at Sun Ship Building and Dry Dock Co. and felt like my old self. Whatever sickness I had was gone. After work, I went home and had a big breakfast, still excited about going up against Satchel and the Monarchs.

That night Shibe Park was packed with my family, friends, and neighbors from Elmwood. Before the game, I was on the bench watching the Stars infield practice when I noticed a stranger handling the catching duties. I also saw three new players who used to be Baltimore Elite Giants—third baseman Felon Snow, pitcher Bill Byrd, and center fielder Henry Kimbro, the same guy I'd thrown out in an earlier game. I turned to Gottlieb's right-hand man, Mike Ianarella, who was sitting near me on the bench. I said, "Mike, what's going on?"

He said, "Don't worry, Bill. You're gonna play."

But when the starting lineup was announced, I found out what was going on.

"Catching for the Stars," the announcer's voice boomed, "is No. 17!" Well, my number was 33. Boy, I saw red. Goose had lured Clarence "Egghead" Clark to catch for the Stars in the biggest game of my young career. This was a slap in the face, especially after the sacrifices I made the day before, playing sick. And here it was, a big game, my relatives and everybody in the stands, and Goose was going to bench me?

I got up, stormed to the clubhouse, and ripped off my uniform. I was steaming when Webster McDonald, the Stars' former coach and founder of my old Daisies team, came into the clubhouse. Mac had become my mentor.

"Bill, whatcha doing?"

"I'm quittin'."

"Whatcha mean, you're quittin'?"

I said, "Mac, yesterday I caught a doubleheader, sick as a dog, and I've been catching for them all year. And they bench me? Today I go out on the field and people in the stands are hollering the names of Baltimore Elite Giant players."

So Mac said, "Bill, let me tell you something. You're a rookie. Make a name for yourself then you can bow out."

So in walked Eddie Gottlieb, the Stars' owner. He wanted to know what my problem was.

"Eddie, I gave you guys my all last night, and now you mistreat me," I said. "My family and all my friends are out there in the stands to see me catch and play against Satchel Paige, and instead you bring in three Elite Giants!"

So Gottlieb thought for a minute and said, "Look, Bill, I'll tear up your contract and give you more money." Now money was usually the quickest way to a ballplayer's heart. But to me, there was more involved, like the team's loyalty to me and my pride. I was still upset, but funny as it seems now, I felt a responsibility to my team, even though they didn't feel a responsibility to me. I slowly slipped back on No. 33 and went to the dugout. I never got in the game.

A year later, I did face Satchel. The Monarchs returned to Philadelphia; the crowd was just as large, and this time, there was no doubt who was catching for the Stars, No. 33, Bill "Ready" Cash.

Now Frank Duncan was doing double-duty for the Monarchs as their catcher and manager. And I remember stepping into the batter's box, and Duncan said to Satchel, "Now, Satchel, you don't know this young man. Don't try to trick him." So I dug in. Satchel went into his all-legs and all-arms windmill windup and threw me a fastball that nipped the outside corner of the plate. I smashed the pitch to right center field on one hop for a triple. I came up again for the second time, caught the third baseman playing back, and laid down a bunt single.

Look, I'm not bragging, but I could always hit Satchel. You just had to stand up in the batter's box and dig in against him. Satchel had such perfect control that he didn't knock you down. So if you stayed in the box and waited for your pitch, you could hit him. One game we beat Satchel 7-2 in Detroit, and I drove in four runs. Oh, and for the record, Kansas City never beat us in Philadelphia while I was with the Stars.

Josh and Satchel were two of the nicest guys you ever wanted to meet. They'd sit down and talk to the rookies about the ins and outs of baseball. Now I know there are a bunch of stories out that Josh drank a lot, and that's why he didn't make it to the majors. Well, from what I saw, drinking wasn't his real problem—women were. Yeah, Josh loved the women, and the women loved Josh Gibson. He "dissipated" a lot—in other words, he ran a lot of women. When you're as friendly and popular as Josh was and belong to the best team in the league, you're probably going to enjoy some, uh, I'll call them, "social benefits."

Me? I was well-behaved. Shoot, I had married the most beautiful girl in the world, so there was no need of me dissipating or staying out late, getting drunk with the fellas. I tried to stay professional throughout my career, on and off the field. And I give Stars coach

Goose Curry credit for at least one thing: he made his players wear a suit and tie whenever we went on the road or played a Sunday game. "You gotta look professional," he'd say.

Between 1943 and 1945, as the war raged and gasoline was rationed, the Stars never played far from Philadelphia. In fact, only the Kansas City Monarchs and the Homestead Grays, the league's marquee teams, traveled any distance to play. I wish I knew how they got gas for their bus. I guess Eddie Gottlieb, who not only owned the Stars, but was also booking agent for every Negro National League team on the East Coast, didn't want to cut into the 10 percent he made per team per game by paying extra for some gasoline.

When we did travel, it was usually by train. Man, we hated to get to Newark to play the Eagles or to Baltimore to play the Elite Giants, because the trains were always full of soldiers, so before or after a game, we couldn't find an empty seat to save our lives and had to stand up until we reached the station. And standing was the last thing you wanted to do, especially after a tough game against those Elite Giants. But if we caught the train in New York City or Washington, D.C., where the trains often originated, the chances of grabbing a seat were better.

Being with the Stars paid me well. I made about three hundred dollars a month playing ball while pulling in about seventy-seven dollars a week at my new job at Sun Ship. Yeah, I got me a new job. The day after I argued with that cracker Jim Bush at Westinghouse, I went to Sun Ship's personnel office and asked for a machinist job. Working in the office was a friend of mine, Charlie Baker. When I told him I was a machinist looking for a good job, he perked up. "We need you," he said. The plant's machine shop hadn't opened because they were still trying to find workers to man it. Well, they had one now.

Sun Ship in those days was going strong. It was the largest shipbuilding company in the world, founded in 1916 by a couple of brothers, J. Howard Pew and Joseph N. Pew Jr. Like its name suggests, Sun Ship was part of the mighty Sun Oil Co.

Man, that place was big, you hear me. It stretched for two miles along the Delaware River in Chester, Pennsylvania. It had twenty-eight ship ways, dozens of cranes, blacksmith shops, pipe and machine shops, fabricating shops, all kinds of shops. At its peak, it employed more than thirty-five thousand people, a bunch of them from Elmwood. It specialized in building oil tankers, and during the war, we were really cranking those babies out. I got a big kick from a newspaper headline from 1943 that said, "Sun Shipyard Builds Tankers Faster Than U-boats Sink Them."

When I arrived, Sun Ship was trying to hire more Negroes to work there. Now this wasn't being done out of the goodness of the Pew brothers' hearts. President Roosevelt had ordered it. He said defense projects had to be integrated. A year before I started work there, Sun Ship wanted to hire nine thousand Negroes to man a new yard and teach them skills like welding, ship fitting, tacking, operating cranes. Remember, back then it was hard for colored people to get one of those good-paying factory and industrial jobs.

Anyway, I got to Sun Ship in March 1943, and like nearly everybody else new, I got put in the "67 Department." I don't remember what the "67" stood for, but people there were sent inside the ships to clean the debris left by welders and other workers. It was a filthy job. I didn't have a locker or any way to clean up after work, so when I got on the trolley car to go home, I sat way in the back where nobody could smell me.

This went on for five weeks. Seemed like every day, they selected two hundred people to send out of "67" to other jobs. For some reason, I kept missing the cut. So I said to this one woman who was a department secretary or something, "Who do I see to get out of here?" I told her if I was going to end up doing this stuff, I wanted my release from Sun Ship.

She said, "Oh, we wouldn't want you to quit." Sun Ship was having a problem keeping welders and machinists because they kept making them do the dirty work inside the ships.

So she sent a note about me to a white guy in a wheelchair. I guess he was a supervisor. He had a nasty attitude and talked to black people like they were dirt. "So ya wanna git outta here?" he said to me.

I said, "Yeah, I want to get out of here. I know my job." Shoot, I was a certified, highly skilled machinist, not some low-level janitor. So he sent me to the "4 Yard," one of Sun Ship's work areas and the yard where colored men were being trained. (Two months after I started at Sun Ship, the SS *Marine Eagle* was launched, the first ocean-going vessel constructed by black men.)

The foreman there was a Jewish guy named Jacobstein. I showed him my machinist certificate, and he said to me, "Cash, glad to have you." Since I just started playing for the Stars, I asked him for a third-shift job so I could play ball in the afternoon and work at night. And he agreed.

I zipped through my training in just one week, and that upset some of the fellas there. They'd tell me, "When they give you a job, it's supposed to last all night." But you know, that was not my style. I had a goal. "I'm looking out for me," I said. "You've been here for a while. I have to make a name for myself."

It worked. I got promoted to the main office where Harry Senick was foreman. He was one of the nicest bosses I ever had. I got to work on the shapers, milling machines, boring mills, and engine lathes. Finally I was doing work I enjoyed and was trained to do.

Now Harry was a big baseball fan, so he took good care of me. I was playing ball and working seven days a week. Those doubleheaders in New York, either at the Polo Grounds or Yankee Stadium, were killers. I usually got home after the games just in time to eat, say hi to Sadie, change my clothes, and catch my ride to Sun Ship. Some nights, I got to work tired as could be.

Those nights, Harry would tell me, "Let me get everybody started." Then he'd take me to a layout table, make sure nobody was watching, then say, "I'll call you," and walk away. I'd curl up underneath the table and fall asleep. Around 4 a.m., lunch time, Harry would return. "Bill, it's time to go," he'd say. I'd wake up, get an assignment, and do it. Like I said, Harry was a nice man, but it worked both ways. He knew I produced for him. I didn't believe in half-stepping. When I got a job to do, I did it well.

I was helping send off two multi-ton ships a month. In my department, we made parts to replace those that broke on machines in the ways. And I could do other jobs as well. I remember one winter night, the snow was about a foot deep, and one of Sun Ship's huge caterpillar cranes got stuck just after the end-of-the-shift whistle blew. Now these cranes could move a ship bow weighing fifty-eight tons. The cable between the wheel and chassis ran out, and they asked me to go out to the crane and see what I could do.

I took two wrenches out there and was back in fifteen minutes. They thought I had come back for more tools. I had come back to go home. "It's working," I told them.

About halfway through 1943, things fell into place. I was playing professional baseball and working as a machinist, making good money. The days of burning old railroad ties for heat and eating white potatoes for dinner were over.

CHAPTER 6

MY FIELDS OF DREAMS AND MVPS

* * *

A ballplayer has two reputations, one with the other players and one with the fans. The first is based on ability. The second the newspapers gives him.
—Johnny Evers, Hall of Fame infielder

I spent seven years with the Philadelphia Stars, some of the most interesting years of my life. Nah, we never contended for a title, but we got to travel around the country and play against the best ballplayers ever.

People sometimes ask me who were the best players in the league, but first I got to tell you about the best places to play. My favorite ball field was Shibe Park, the Monday home of the Stars. Like they say, there's no place like home, and when we played, we packed that stadium. If the A's and Phillies had ten thousand people on a Sunday, that was a big crowd for them. We'd come in on Monday night and cram about forty thousand in a stadium that only seated 34,500. Shoot, our fans stood all over the place.

My least favorite place to play was Bugle Field in Baltimore, the home of the Elite Giants. Man, we hated that "bowl in the hole." It was always hot as hell, and the outfield had a ten-foot rise, giving the field the shape of a bowl. And you know what made it worse? The Elite Giants was one of the best teams in the league. Shoot, they'd run your butt ragged. Plus they had Bill Byrd, one of the only two pitchers in the league allowed to throw spitballs. The other guy was Nick Stanley with the New York Black Yankees.

Let me tell you something, Byrd really loaded it up too. He'd work up a big ball of saliva in his mouth, raise his glove with the ball inside, and spit into it. Then he'd wind up, rear back, and fire that spitter. At first the ball didn't look like it was doing nothing special— it just came straight at you. But when you swung at it, man, that ball dropped like a ton of bricks. And if you were lucky enough to hit it, that spit splattered all over you.

The umps let Stanley and Byrd throw spitters because they were the only ones who could control the pitch. Thank goodness I never had to catch a spitball pitcher. If somebody was trying to take a base on me and I had to handle one of those slippery balls, I'd probably throw it all the way into center field.

Man, we played real aggressive, exciting games in the Negro Leagues. We loved to bunt for hits, hit-and-run, and steal. Our fans loved the way we played. And thank goodness for black newspapers. They didn't always keep the best stats or most accurate information, but they did keep our names in front of the public and kept the league alive. Fans voted for the East-West teams using coupons found in their newspapers. And the newspapers hyped that game like the Super Bowl is hyped today. They were papers like the *Philadelphia Tribune, Pittsburgh Courier, Chicago Defender*, the *Amsterdam News* in New

York, and of course, *The Afro-American* in the Baltimore-Washington area.

You know, prior to Jackie's entry into the majors, some Negro columnists like Frank Young at the *Chicago Defender* and Chester Washington at the *Courier* were leading the change for integration. And once Jackie got in, Negro writers like Sam Lacy and Wendell Smith followed his every move. In Philly, W. Rollo Wilson of the *Tribune* followed us Stars. And a youngster named Malcolm Poindexter, who later became the dean of black television reporters in Philadelphia, also covered us.

So you want to know who the best players were? Well, here's my list. Some of these guys you may have never heard of. Others are well known. And you can disagree all you want, but I stand by them.

Josh Gibson: The greatest hitter ever.

Satchel Paige: The greatest pitcher ever.

Hilton Smith: A close second to Satch. He played on the Monarchs with Satch and was one of six right-handers on the team. When Kansas City came to town, we always wanted to know who was going to pitch after Satchel, because Satchel pitched only about three innings a game. We knew we could get runs off Connie Johnson, Ford Smith, or any of those other guys. But Hilton Smith? Shoot, he had everything—a fastball that moved, a curve, a slider, and change of pace that left you in knots. When Hilton was on the mound, he was like another infielder. Plus the guy could hit.

Leon Day: When Leon wasn't pitching for the Newark Eagles, he'd play second base, shortstop, outfield, everywhere.

Verdell "Lefty" Mathis: Ace left-hander for the Memphis Red Sox.

Larry Doby: Second baseman for the Newark Eagles. He hit .408 in our league and ran like a deer so they sometimes put him in the outfield. The Cleveland Indians signed Larry in 1947, making him the first Negro to play in the American League. I remember playing against him in Ruppert Stadium, in one of his last games as a Negro Leaguer. "I'm glad to see you go," I said to him, "because we could never get you out." Larry was a heck of a ballplayer, but in my opinion, he really didn't play his best when he first joined Cleveland. It was like he was shy of the white players. But when he got a black roommate, right fielder Harry "Suitcase" Simpson, Larry broke out in a big way. Larry got into the Hall of Fame in 1998, and he deserved it.

Art Pennington: Know what his nickname was? "Superman." And for a good reason. He played right field for the Chicago American Giants and, with his tremendous arm, easily threw out runners at home plate. And man, he was built—like Superman. Plus the women loved Art. We were the one-two punch on the Culiacan team of the Mexican Pacific Coast League. I mean, if a runner was on second and the ball was hit to Art in right, I'd whip off my mask and just stand there, ready to tag out the base runner rounding third because I knew Art would make a perfect, one-hop throw to me at home. After a while, the guys got smart. When a ball went to Art in right, they didn't even try to score. Art and I got close during our years in baseball.

Frank Austin: My fellow Star. He played shortstop in my rookie year. Austin was actually Panamanian, not an American Negro. But that didn't make no difference. He was excellent. He only stayed in the league for a year or two before signing for more money to play in the Pacific Coast League.

Webster McDonald: Like I said before, Webster was the only manager to take the Stars to a championship. A former pitcher, he later became a father figure to me.

Roy Partlow: Another pitcher. He was with the Homestead Grays. Branch Rickey signed him two weeks before Jackie Robinson to play in the minors. But Roy believed in "an eye for an eye." He was in Montreal when Jackie was there preparing to break into the majors. When Jackie was in some of those Southern cities, guys used to throw at him. Roy would tell Jackie, "Don't worry about it. My time's coming." And when it was his turn to pitch, Roy would knock those guys down. He got shipped to Nashua, New Hampshire, where Roy Campanella and Don Newcombe were, and went 17-1 one year.

Roy Campanella: A catcher for the Baltimore Elite Giants and the Brooklyn Dodgers, Campy was another guy who didn't back down. I remember we were playing the Giants at Forty-fourth and Parkside one year, leading 4-1 in the ninth. We had a rookie named Woods playing second base, and he didn't know how to pivot on a double play. Now Campy was the runner on first. A ground ball gets hit to Frank Austin at short, who throws the ball to Woods, who catches it, turns to throw it to first, but gets knocked into center field by Campy. I swear, Campy comes into second base like a runaway truck and hits Woods high with a football block.

"Camp, that's dirty," I yelled at him. "This is baseball, not football!"

Do you know what he said to me? "He was in the way. I'm trying to save the game."

Yeah, save the game—my foot. I don't know what was wrong with Campy. I always believed that the way a person acts has something to do with his upbringing and the way he was treated in the past. I don't know everything about Campy's past, except that he was born in Philadelphia, so I won't be too quick to judge. All I know is that when he was in our league, he was a mean son of a gun.

Raul Galata: This kid pitched for the Indianapolis Clowns and shut us out three straight games. He pitched the last game I played with the Stars in Shibe Park. Born in 1930 in Cuba, he never made it to organized ball, preferring to play in the Pacific Coast League. But, man, he was good.

Dave "Skinny" Barnhill: He was the ace pitcher for the New York Cubans. He let his fingernails grow long so he could use them to cut the seams in a baseball. And those fingernail cuts changed the ball's trajectory. If the air's on top, the ball's going to drop. If the air is on the bottom, it's going to rise. So that ball winds up dancing all around the plate, and the batter can't figure out what's going on.

I caught "Skinny" during the East-West game. He threw nine pitches, each one for a strike. Later we were teammates in Cuba, where I caught him for fifteen innings in a 0-0 game that was suspended because the rules said we couldn't complete a game after midnight. To protect Dave and our team, I'd throw the ball back to him as fast as I could so the ump couldn't see all the cuts he had put in the ball. And the batters, well, they didn't notice anything different, they just figured they missed the ball.

Really, Dave was good enough that he didn't have to cut the ball. At a gathering of Negro Leaguers a few years ago, we all laughed along with Skinny about how many balls he'd cut up. In one game when he was with the Minneapolis Millers of the American Association, the umpire threw out twenty-four balls that Skinny had dug his fingernails into. "Those were some big guys coming to the plate with their big bats," Skinny said, explaining why he had cut up so many of them. "I had to use something to keep them from hitting the ball."

One guy you won't find on my MVP list is pitcher **Don Newcombe** of the Newark Eagles and later the Brooklyn Dodgers. He was gutless. Once Newcombe was pitching against us at Shibe Park. Our shortstop, Frank Austin, was a good hitter, so Newcombe always threw directly at him so he couldn't hit nothing. And that ticked us off. But Stars pitcher Roy Partlow wouldn't get too concerned. "That's all right," he said. "Let him do it. I'll get 'im back."

So when Newcombe came up to bat, Partlow threw his fastball right behind Newcombe, scaring the you-know-what out of him. And do you know what Newcombe did? He went over to the Eagles manager and asked to be taken out of the game because "his arm hurt." Yeah, right. That guy never stayed a full game against us, as scared as he was. All we did was practice simple baseball etiquette: throw at our man, you're going down on your butt.

I played every position on the Stars except pitcher and shortstop. I felt nobody—black, white, red, or green—could out-throw, out-hit, or out-run me. Try to steal? Shoot, get that ball to me and there was a better-than-average chance I'd throw the runner out. One major league catcher told my friend Jimmy Dean, a pitcher for the Stars, "I wish I had an arm like Cash. Nobody would run on me."

Yeah, I was confident in my skills. And when I played, I hustled. Shoot, I could never understand guys who put on a uniform and loafed.

CHAPTER 7

TRYING TO ADJUST

* * *

The price one pays for pursuing any profession, or calling, is an intimate knowledge of its ugly side.
— Writer James Baldwin

In 1944, Sadie and I had a daughter, Janet, who increased the size of our family to four. Let me tell you, Janet got my determination and my wife's good looks. (Thank goodness she didn't get mine.) But shortly after her birth, things got a little tense in the Cash household. My being away so much playing ball finally got to my Sadie. Lonely, restless, and longing to have a job, Sadie one day told me she wanted to enroll in the Apex Beauty College on Broad Street where colored women learned to become beauticians. I got to admit I wasn't thrilled with the idea and told her so. I mean, Janet was just six months old, for goodness sakes, and she and Bill Jr. needed their mother at home. But Sadie wanted to do hair.

Now, for colored women around this time, doing hair was a big deal and a way to make good money. I mean, hair care by the '40s had become serious business for black people. You got to give credit to that woman named Annie Turnbo Malone, who created some stuff for black hair. I think it was called Poro products or something like that. And you had Madame C.J. Walker who, around the early 1900s, created that Walker hair-straightening system. It used a hair-grower, shampoo, hot iron combs, and vigorous brushing to make colored people's nappy hair straight, almost like white folks. The story goes that Walker was the first woman, white or black, to become a millionaire without getting money passed to her from some rich husband or other relative. In fact, her success got other women, like Madame Sarah Spencer Washington, to create the Apex schools.

Anyway, when I came home from work that day, Sadie wasn't there, and Mom and Dad broke the news to me: Sadie was in beauty school and had left Janet with the neighbors. I was a bit ticked by that; obviously my tough talk had no impact on my wife. But I knew when I was licked. So I went to the neighbor's house, picked up Janet, and dressed her up real nice. Then the two of us went on down to the Apex school to pay Sadie a surprise visit and take her out to lunch. From that day on, if I had the day off from work, I'd go to the school and treat Sadie to lunch.

I had a car, so I didn't use public transportation at the time, but something occurred that year that caused a lot of trouble for folks who rode the buses in Philadelphia. So much trouble that President Roosevelt had to send in the troops.

See, in August 1944, the white workers of the Philadelphia Transportation Co., which we called PTC, went on strike because they didn't want blacks as drivers. The black PTC workers wanted equality; they could do all the menial jobs but weren't allowed to handle the high-profile and responsible job of driving trolleys and buses—it was the same sort of thing I faced at Westinghouse. The NAACP and other groups supported the black workers. In fact, in 1943, the federal government had ordered PTC to integrate. But when eight blacks passed a written exam and were training to become drivers a year later, six thousand white PTC employees couldn't stomach the thought and—against their union's wishes—walked out on August 1.

Man, it wasn't pretty. Recalling those days, William Barber, one of the blacks who passed the test, told *Philadelphia Daily News* reporter Frank Dougherty back in 1994, "The white drivers said they definitely did not want blacks on the trolley cars or buses because [blacks] were inferior, they smelled, they carried a certain amount of disease, and just about anything they could possibly say about a black." Well, this was the middle of World War II, and Philadelphia was an important city when it came to producing goods and services for the war. But the wildcat strike, along with the gasoline rationing, made it hard for people who had jobs to get to work.

So FDR sent in the troops, five thousand of them, to be exact. They had rifles, light artillery, .30-caliber machine guns, arrest powers, and they weren't playing. The troops protected the buses, trolleys, and depots—they rode the buses and trolleys carrying rifles and ammunition—and the army, commanded by Maj. Gen. Philip Hayes, threatened to revoke the strikers' occupational draft deferments. Five days into the strike, four ringleaders were fired, and the troops ran the city's transportation system.

The army returned control to PTC on August 17, but some whites had a tough time watching a black man drive their buses and trolleys. Barber said some of them would buy trolley car tokens, which were two for fifteen cents back then. But instead of giving it to the operator, they'd throw them on the floor and leave the car. Man, we black folks have had to struggle for so much.

A National Guardsman watches over a white female passenger on a trolley during the Philadelphia Transportation Co. strike of 1944. (Credit: Temple University Libraries, Urban Archives, Philadelphia, Pa.)

To me, 1945 was the Stars' best year that I was with them. And as was always the case in the Negro Leagues, it was one of the strangest years too.

We had a darn good club. Benson, as usual, was our leader and helped the young players adjust to the league. I still remember my rookie year when the Eagles' Roy "Red" Parnell cursed me out for some reason. I'm slow to boil, but when I get steamed, watch out! I had heard enough of Parnell's mouth and went after him with a bat. That's right, a bat. I was hot. But Benson quickly stepped in between us and calmed me down.

Pitcher Barney Brown and first baseman Jim West were my close friends on the team, and I had a good relationship with pitchers Joe Fillmore and Bill Ricks. We stayed pretty much to ourselves while the other guys were a little wilder and did their share of what we called "dissipating."

Before the 1945 season started, there was the usual talk of whether the Negro League would survive, especially with the majors showing more interest in bringing blacks into their league. Many white starting players were getting drafted for the war, diluting the major league talent pool. W. Rollo Wilson, in one of his *Tribune* columns, said black players should "apply for employment" on the Brooklyn and Boston major league teams. But he knew the reality. "A one-armed man, a one-legged man, Cubans, Chinese, Mexicans—anyone except a known colored man is welcomed into the big leagues at this time."

You know, there was always some issue hanging over our league. Wilson wondered whether the Negro League owners would put aside their petty differences and concentrate on making the league stronger. For instance, there was bickering about the financial setup of the East-West game. And then there was this new United States League.

Branch Rickey and Gus Greenlee were at the forefront of this league. It was sort of a minor league for Negro players. But these teams would be owned by blacks and whites alike. See, Rickey had it all figured out. He could scout teams in the Negro Leagues, saying he was looking for players for a team called the Brooklyn Brown Dodgers, managed by Oscar Charleston, who worked at the Quartermasters in Philadelphia. We know now this league camouflaged Rickey's real goal: To find just the right black man to bring into the major leagues.

Stanley Glenn, my backup on the Stars, played for the Brown Dodgers, and I got them to sign outfielder Jimmy "Chip" Wilkes. I knew Jimmy from the neighborhood, and I knew he was good and fast and knew he wasn't working. So I brought him, two balls, and a fungo bat over to a field near the Quartermasters for a tryout with Oscar. You should've seen Chip. He was catching balls like Willie Mays would a few years later. I mean he was making basket catches in front of him, over the shoulder, all kinds of great plays. Oscar didn't need much more convincing and signed Chip up.

The United States League had eight teams, but only for a second. After Rickey found Jackie Robinson, the league folded in the middle of 1945. Just like that. I tried to get Goose to sign Chip to the Stars, but Goose wasn't interested. "He's too little," Goose said to me.

The next day, we went to Newark to play the Eagles, and guess who was in center field for them? Jimmy "Chip" Wilkes. And he wasn't so little in this game. He smacked that ball all over the field. The Eagles had Johnny Davis in left and Bob Harvey in right. Davis was really an Indian who could cover balls hit down the foul line, but that was about it. And Harvey? Shoot, he was so big he could only cover the part of the outfield he was standing in. But they were both great home-run hitters so they were in the lineup. And so Jimmy told them, "Y'all just take care of the line. I'll take care of left center and right center." And he did. Man, could he fly!

And how about W. Rollo Wilson, the newspaper columnist? Even he was optimistic about our chances in 1945. "Little change is anticipated in the makeup of the Philly Stars this season, according to advance word from a [Ed] Bolden, spokesman," Wilson wrote in early April.

"Most cheering to manager Homer 'The Goose' Curry is that Frank Austin has signed his contract and will arrive from Panama about the middle of this month. Their freshman shortstop ... was the 1944 sensation of the league. He led in loop batting and was one of the best fielding shortstops in the game."

Benson, Jim West, Bill Ricks, and Barney Brown were also coming back. And Wilson had some kind words about me. "Bill Cash, who improved in 1944 more than any other local player, will be back as first-string catcher."

Wilson kept the heat on the Negro Leagues and what might happen if blacks were finally brought into the majors. He saw what was coming down the pike—the breakup of the Negro Leagues. He called Eddie Bolden a "nabob" because Eddie said the Negro League would get stronger if blacks were let into the majors.

"The Negro League players would give you their best effort for they would know that they were in a position to make the big leagues, and to get in they would have to be on their toes at all times," Bolden told Wilson.

Goose said his team was "ready and willing to go." And our fans had another reason to be excited. The field at Forty-fourth and Parkside got a partial facelift. Some of the stands were rebuilt and new screens installed.

We had six teams in our division that year. Besides us, there were the Washington Homestead Grays, Baltimore Elite Giants, Newark Eagles, New York Cubans, and New York Black Yankees. On opening day, May 5, we slaughtered the Giants 13-0, banging out sixteen hits. The papers said I wasn't in the lineup, but I sure don't remember that. The next day, we split a doubleheader with the Giants, losing the first 6-2 and winning the second shortened game, 8-5. I had a home run in both games in front of a crowd of six thousand. Or at least that's the number they put in the papers. Shoot, you really couldn't believe those guys when it came to attendance figures because team owners had a lot at stake by keeping those numbers low: the fewer people in "official" attendance, the less the owners had to pay us and the more they kept in their own darn pockets.

And if there was one day when owners raked in a lot of cash, it was on Memorial Day. See, in the Negro Leagues, Memorial Day was special, like a major holiday. The adults were off from work, the kids out of school. So they all celebrated by going to the ballpark and watching us play. And the Negro League team owners figured, shoot, they could make a killing at the gate by having the teams play several games in different cities. So on Memorial Day 1945, we again were playing the Elite Giants. In the afternoon, we split a doubleheader at Forty-fourth and Parkside, losing the first 5-4, winning a shortened second game, 2-0. Then we got on the bus and traveled south to Blue Rock Park in Wilmington, Del., for our third game in less than twelve hours, and beat the Eagles 9-4. After that game, man, we were dead tired.

Now some people may try to talk about how wonderful the Negro Leagues were and stuff, and to be honest, we did play some good ball and entertained our fans and scratched out a decent living. But just like everything else, the Negro Leagues were a business. So what happened to us in 1945 shouldn't have come as a surprise, but it still hurt like all get out.

See, Eddie Gottlieb owned the Stars. But he was also booking agent for all the Negro League teams that came from the East. And you know something? He didn't even want his own team, the Stars, in the Negro League championship game. And neither did the league. It wanted a team with a bunch of big-name stars that could draw people from all over. They wanted the Homestead Grays; you know, with Cool Papa Bell, Josh, and the guys. So just like that, the league threw out several of our wins, making us something like 7-10 and turning the Grays from runners-up to second-half Negro National League division champs. The Grays suddenly were 14-6 and faced the Negro American League division champs, the Cleveland Buckeyes, with catcher Quincy Trouppe and infielder Parnell Woods in the black World Series.

But God don't like ugly, and the Grays got their comeuppance—they lost to the Buckeyes in four straight. I'm not going to lie; we felt bad about getting screwed like that, but what could we do, you know? That's how it worked in the Negro Leagues. And we were so eager to play ball we put up with just about anything, including this crazy way of setting up championship games. This was one reason the majors didn't take us seriously. Plus it didn't help that bookies and other shady characters owned some of the teams.

At that time, there were only four teams in the Negro Leagues set up like those in the majors, you know, with a strong organizational structure and some stability. They were the Chicago American Giants, the Monarchs, the Memphis Red Sox, and the Birmingham Black Barons. The Red Sox were owned by the four Martin brothers, each one a doctor, and each was known by his initials. They were J.B., A.T., W.S., and B.B. Memphis also had its own field named—what else—Martin Park, which meant the Red Sox didn't have to share a major league stadium or play in a minor league park. Kansas City also had its own place. For a Negro League team to have its own stadium was a big deal, especially to us players.

In this 1946 Philadelphia Stars team photograph, Bill is standing on the second row, second from the end. That's team owner Ed Bolden in the middle, in suit, tie and hat. (Credit: From The Cash/Thompson Collection, Courtesy of The African American Museum in Philadelphia.)

After that screwing we got in '45, you'd figure '46 couldn't be no worse, right? Well, it was. They say bad things happen in threes, and sure enough, first I was laid off from Sun Ship in March. Then I missed a chance to play with the Satchel Paige All-Stars. And third, to top it off, I got suspended because they said I punched an umpire. And I swear that umpire thing was an accident, a pure and simple accident. I mean, if they had had real umps at that game, it may not have happened.

The Stars were in Newark, New Jersey, playing the Eagles in Ruppert Stadium. It was May 5, opening day of the season. The stadium had eight thousand charged-up Eagles fans who believed their team was due to finally win a championship. Several of their stars were back from the service, like infielder Clarence "Pint" Israel, outfielder Monte Irvin, and pitcher Leon Day. During the off-season, the Eagles' owners made an unpopular trade, giving us infielder Murray Watkins in return for infielder Pat Patterson.

Anyway, Day was on the mound, enjoying lousy calls by a white, part-time ump identified in newspaper clips as Peter Strauch. Hell, I didn't know his name; I just know he was really screwing us during the game. Nobody can tell me that Eagles owner Effa Manley didn't offer him a little something extra to cheat us. It seemed like every call went against us. The darn ball's up over our heads, Strauch called a strike. Ball's way outside, he called a strike. The ball hit us, he called a strike. Man, we *had* to swing at bad pitches just to improve our chances of a decent at-bat. But the Eagles? Shoot, if the ball was in the heart of the plate and they didn't swing, he called it a ball.

It was the bottom of the sixth and no score. Our pitcher, lefty Barney Brown, was doing a great job despite the ump's antics. The Eagles scored when Israel tripled off the right center field wall, and Larry Doby smacked a single to center, driving him home. Doby tagged and went to second on a fly out. One out. Then came the play.

Doby was on second when Irvin slapped a slow one-hopper to shortstop Frank Austin. Frank threw to first baseman Wesley "Doc" Dennis, who tagged his bag and fired the ball to me.

Now here came Doby, huffing and puffing from second base, rounding third and heading home on a routine ground out. He was halfway down the third-base line. I caught the ball from Doc, turned, and went up the line to meet Doby. He hit the dirt on his stomach, arms and legs stretched out, trying to slide headfirst into home plate. I hit the dirt on my stomach too, blocking the plate and making the tag. I'm telling you, the plate was at least four feet behind me.

The ump called him safe. I was like, just beside myself.

"Whaaaatt?!" I yelled, and when I thrust my arms up in protest, my gloved hand caught Strauch right under his chin, knocking him backward to the ground. Shoot, the call was so bad that Goose came running in from right field and kicked Strauch in the butt while the ump was still on the ground.

The ump sputtered, "You...you...you kicked me!"

"I didn't do it," Goose said, trying to sound innocent and stuff. Then Goose started mouthing off at the guy.

Well, things got crazy. Stars swarmed in from the field and off the bench and gave me let's call it "moral support" by yelling at Strauch. Then some fans ran onto the field. Then the Newark cops came and needed thirty minutes to bring things back to normal. I got kicked out of the game and wasn't allowed back in the dugout. And Goose? He was so ticked off that the cops had to grab him by his uniform and lead him off the field.

In the controversial play, a sliding Larry Doby appears to be shy of home plate as Bill puts the tag on him. (Credit: Moorland-Spingarn Research Center, Howard University.)

Oh, the papers had a field day. The play made the front of the *New York Amsterdam News* under the headline, "Police Halt Philadelphia Stars-Newark Eagles Riot." Now I wouldn't call it a riot, but things did get a little testy. And while I'm at it, let me clear up a few errors that are more than sixty years old, OK?

A couple of stories about that play said Doby tried to score after the Eagles' Lenny Pearson hit a grounder to Duckett, our second baseman. That's not what happened. Actually it was Irvin who hit the grounder to Austin at short. Look, I was there and that play is burned in my memory forever. And I didn't "attack" the umpire; I don't care what those newspapers said.

And another thing. The Eagles won 2-0, but on top of the bad umpiring, even the scorer was against us. The record books said Leon Day pitched a no-hitter that day. He didn't pitch a no-hitter. He actually pitched a one-hitter, but the scorer changed that hit to an error (one of two credited to young shortstop Gil Fielder) to preserve the no-hitter for Day. Can you believe that? But, hey, we were playing in Newark, and this was, after all, the Negro Leagues.

I took a big hit because of that game. I got suspended for three games and fined twenty-five dollars. A photograph of the play taken by Chick Solomon of the *New York Amsterdam News* bore me out—Doby was out and Strauch had messed up. We even took the photo to the league office. Lot of good that did. Those umps weren't professional, just some losers brought in by the Eagles' owners. And to be honest, that wasn't unusual. With so many teams going, the league was unable to provide each game with legitimate umps, so the home teams often provided their own. Lloyd "Pepper" Bassett, who caught for a bunch of Negro League teams, had said, "There was no umpiring, only guessing." And I say amen to that.

Some people think the reason I didn't make it to the majors was because I smacked that white ump. I'm not dismissing the notion. Fred McCreary was the league's umpire chief and one of the best legitimate umps around. He was always picked for the East-West game. Well, he was sitting in our dugout that day of the play. He was supposed to ump a game in Yankee Stadium, but it was rained out. So he caught the train to Newark to watch our game. He saw the play. He said I should've stomped Strauch.

That Eagles win was a sign of the good things to come for the team. After starting hot, the Eagles slumped. Abe

Manley and manager Biz Mackey made some lineup
changes, and the Eagles came to life. They won fourteen
or fifteen in June—those last two wins on June 30 came
at our expense, when they swept us in a doubleheader in
Newark, with Day and right-hander Rufus Lewis tossing
shutouts—and finished the season's first half in first place
with a 25-9 record. At one time we were in first place too,
but finished second at 17-12 in the six-team division.

According to James Overmyer, author of *Effa Manley
and the Newark Eagles*, the 1946 Eagles had a batting
average of .301 and forty-six home runs in fifty-nine
games. The leading batter was Irvin with .394, then Doby
with .342. Three other batters had averages between
.330 and .340. And no team can go anywhere without
a strong pitching staff. Max Manning was 11-1, and Day
was 11-4 with 105 strikeouts.

The Eagles rolled into the second half, going 22-7
and winning the Negro National League Pennant. To
get ready for the black World Series against the Kansas
City Monarchs, Effa bought the Eagles new white home
uniforms, Overmyer said, and for the opening game in
Newark on September 19, she had heavyweight boxing
champ Joe "The Brown Bomber" Louis throw out the
first ball.

The series—played in Newark, Kansas City, Comiskey
Park in Chicago, and the New York Polo Grounds—
went seven games. There were a couple of blowouts in
Kansas City—the Monarchs won 15-5 in Game 3; the
Eagles won 8-1 in Game 4—but the deciding game in
Newark was close, and the Monarchs played without
three of their best players.

The way my friend Buck O'Neil told it in his book
I Was Right on Time, Willard Brown, who had one of

the hottest bats in the league, missed the game. So did outfielder Ted Strong. Buck said they went into New York that day to sign contracts to play winter ball in Puerto Rico and didn't make it back to Newark until the game was over. They told Buck and the boys they had gotten caught in traffic. And guess who else was missing? Satch. Now Satch usually made it a habit to arrive at games late, but this time he didn't even bother to show up at all. Still, the Eagles won 3-2.

In September of that year, Satch was supposed to come east to give out the names of players on his all-star team. My name was on that list. The Satchel Paige All-Stars were going to play a team of white major leaguers led by Cleveland pitcher Bob Feller in Comiskey Park in Chicago. Well, three days before Satchel's announcement, the Stars were playing the Monarchs at Griffith Stadium in Washington. Earl Taborn, the Monarch catcher, fouled off a ball that slammed into my right thumb, breaking it. So I couldn't go with Satch. Lou Louden from the New York Cubans went instead. Yeah, I was a little ticked I couldn't go.

Even though my finger was still stiff, I played in an all-star game in Maracaibo, Venezuela, around the first part of November. The only reason I mention this is because it was the first year I played both winter and summer baseball. Most Negro League players chose to play ball during the two seasons. But I really had no choice—I'd been laid off at Sun Ship, and my family needed the money.

So I went to play for the Vargas team from Caracas, the capital of Venezuela. I remember we were in a seven-game series with Maracaibo when one of the Vargas team owners bet fifteen thousand dollars that his own team would lose. Now if that wasn't the dumbest thing. The deciding game was tied 0-0 for six innings. In the seventh, Parnell Woods, who had played third base for the Cleveland Buckeyes, and Marvin Williams, the Stars second baseman, hit back-to-back home runs, and we went into the ninth leading 2-0.

In the top of the inning, Maracaibo punched out three straight singles, bringing one run across the plate. One pop out later, there were runners on first and third. So I got a little worried, and since I was the catcher, I was trying to figure out how to get out of this problem. I scanned the field then walked to the mound to talk to Henry Miller. "Henry, give me a good curveball and we'll get out of this mess," I said. I settled in behind the plate; Henry fired a perfect curve, and the Maracaibo batter beat the ball into the ground to shortstop Luis Aparacio—man, he could really pick it—who handled it with ease and turned it into a game-ending double play. We won 2-1.

And the owner who bet against us? He couldn't pay up. Right after the game, he blew his brains out with a .45. Stupid.

Also that winter, the Yankees came to Caracas to play against us. The major league guys loved coming to Latin America because the pay was good, the weather nice, and the competition stiff. The Yankees didn't bring "Joltin'" Joe DiMaggio because he was recovering from a foot operation. They did have a young Yogi Berra, though, who had just joined the team as an outfielder. Hilton Smith was pitching for us and kept the game close. In one inning, a fly ball was hit to Yogi in right. He circled under and confidently yelled, "I got it! I got it!" Man, that ball dropped twenty feet behind him.

We trailed 3-2 before Lloyd "Ducky" Davenport—we called him "Ducky" because, well, he ran like a duck—an outfielder for the Buckeyes, smacked a fastball off, I believe, Allie Reynolds. Cliff Mapes broke in on the ball then watched helplessly as Venezuela's high altitude allowed the line drive to sail over his head. The home run won the game for us, 4-3. Until then, the Yankees had beaten every team they played during their barnstorming swing. And Yogi's outfield blunder that day may have convinced the Yankees to make him a full-time catcher instead.

Between games in Caracas, we had a lot of down time. I mean, we were in a foreign country, so there was only so much we could do. Some of my teammates, usually led by Sam Bankhead, liked to spend the empty hours drinking. They'd get a fifth of Johnnie Walker Red, six Cokes, and just get toasted. They knew I didn't drink, but they'd still ask me to join them. They weren't trying to just be friendly—they wanted me to help pay for the drinks. No dice.

After playing in Venezuela, where the color of a player's skin wasn't important, I was rudely reminded on my return to the United States that I was black. My flight out of Caracas on Eastern Airlines stopped over in Jacksonville, Florida, where this white woman boarded. You could tell right away she was a cracker, acting all snooty, like her stuff didn't stink. She came down the aisle and told the stewardess that she wanted my seat. There were twenty-one people in the DC-4, which seated fifty-four, the plane was barely half full, and she wanted my seat.

"I'm sorry. That's Mr. Cash's seat," the stewardess said.

"Humph," the woman muttered and walked away.

Having that white stewardess stand up for me meant a lot. I thanked her, and since then, I always took Eastern whenever I flew.

To me, the Negro Leagues suffered its greatest loss on January 20, 1947. I remember a couple of my Vargas teammates and I, including Sam and Hilton Smith, were in a Caracas hotel lobby playing pinochle when a hotel bellhop walked through shouting, "Bankhead! Telegram! Bankhead! Telegram!"

Sam called the bellhop over, opened up the telegram, slowly read it, and then quietly shared the news with us. "Josh is dead," he said. The greatest hitter ever died of a stroke at age thirty-six in Pittsburgh.

The great Josh Gibson of the Homestead Grays at bat with Bill behind the plate, around 1944-45. (Credit: Art Carter Papers, Prints and Photographs Department, Moorland-Spingarn Research Center, Howard University.)

You know, the last few years of his life, Josh Gibson had health problems, like blackouts, headaches, and bouts of dizziness. In '42 or '43, doctors discovered he had a brain tumor, but Josh reportedly wouldn't let them cut on him.

But some people speculate he was really hurt when Jackie Robinson—and not one of the real stars of the Negro Leagues like Josh, Satchel, or Cool Papa—got to break the major league color barrier. I don't know about that. I do know Josh was a heck of a player and a heck of a person.

Man, Josh's death devastated us—I mean devastated us. And those who were really close to him took it hard. Sam, our manager and Josh's teammate on the Homestead Grays back in the 1930s, just went off.

Funny. The day before we learned Josh died, Sam had had a terrific game—and I mean a terrific game. We played a team of Venezuelans, and Sam was in center, nursing a sore arm he hurt pitching the previous game. Center field was our weak spot, and we had to win this game, so we took a chance and put Sam out there. Even hurt, he was way better than the guy who usually played there.

We were leading 2-1 in the ninth when one of their players got on and was bunted to second. Then their No. 4 batter—man, he could hit—slammed a blistering ball up the middle. I ripped off my catcher's mask and tossed it aside. *If Sam wants him,* I said to myself, *he can have him.*

Sure enough, Sam scooped up the ball on one hop and fired it—sore arm and all—into the infield. The ball ricocheted off the back of the mound and skipped right into my mitt. We nailed the base runner at the plate and won the game.

Sam and Josh had been real tight. When he learned Josh was dead, Sam went out and returned hours later drunk as I don't know what. Sam stumbled into his hotel room and flew into a rage, tearing up furniture, breaking things, screaming, and sobbing.

Sam's pain ran deep. They had to send him home.

CHAPTER 8

BREAKING DOWN THE DOOR

✳ ✳ ✳

Baseball has done a lot for the Negro, but the Negro has done more for baseball.
—Larry Doby, first Negro player in the
American League

When I returned to the Stars in the spring of 1947, Jackie was playing for the Brooklyn Dodgers, the first colored man in sixty-three years to play in the all-white majors. Before that, catcher Moses Fleetwood Walker and later his brother, Welday, had played for the Toledo, Ohio Blue Stockings in the American Association, one of three baseball leagues considered "major" way back in 1884. But that would be the last time Negroes played with whites in major league baseball—until Jackie did.

Jackie played for the Kansas City Monarchs in 1945. Most of us Negro Leaguers liked Jackie, but he hated playing with us. He'd been a big-time college athlete, a four-sport star, an officer in the service. So he was used to much better living and playing conditions.

Jackie was a man of style. He could stand up to abuse and name-calling but still stay focused on the ball. He kept the feisty side of his personality in check for a few years, in an agreement with Dodger president Branch

Rickey, but turned that anger into a kind of inner resolve to do well for himself and his race.

Jackie was quick and daring. But I knew the real reason why Rickey brought him into the majors: money.

You know, I feel sorry for this country because everything seems to come down to what'll make money, not what's morally right. The Negro Leagues had a lot of fans in the '30s and '40s. The greedy major league team owners wanted them, but none had the guts to take the step Rickey took. The reason why we had such loyal fans was because we were good and played a more exciting and entertaining game than white folks. You want proof? Just look at what happened when we played against the major leaguers barnstorming in North America or in Mexico or Latin America. I'd say 75 percent of the major league ballplayers couldn't play in our league.

Those celebrations in 1997, marking the fiftieth anniversary of Jackie's entry into the major leagues, were wonderful, man. More blacks have become the stars: Bobby Bonds and Ken Griffey Jr. But if you ask me, there's still a lot of prejudice, especially when it comes to putting blacks in management and front-office positions.

However, in 1947, my concern was being the best catcher in the league, not change the world like Jackie did. Two years prior, Uncle Sam dropped the A-bomb on Hiroshima and Nagasaki, forcing Japan to surrender, ending World War II and freeing gasoline restrictions. So the Stars had their own bus, and traveling was no longer a problem.

Man, riding in the bus was rough, especially if we didn't shower after a game. The smell on that bus could be something else. The back seat was reserved for uniforms, bags, and other equipment, so we were cramped in our seats. But I got to tell you, the most brutal trips came when we traveled down south. Before those trips, we went to the grocery store and loaded up on bread, bologna, and cheese for sandwiches. We had to eat while on the road because down south, the white owners and managers of the diners and restaurants refused to let us eat in them.

I went into the 1947 season with high hopes. There was one game when one of our pitchers walked six men, and I picked four of them off first base. Something happened that year that showed how greed could affect ballplayers' careers.

But first, let me tell you a little about Stanley Glenn. Stanley lived in Elmwood and was my backup on the Stars. As a matter of fact, I was responsible for him being on the team. I used to see him play at Bartram High School. Back in '44, I told Goose that I couldn't catch all of the exhibition games, all of the league games, and work too. We needed a backup. So I sent Goose over to Bartram's field at Fifty-eighth Street and Elmwood Avenue, where Stanley was playing his last high school game. Stanley had a home run, a double, and a single. The Stars signed him on the spot.

The next morning, Stanley was on my doorstep, excited and ready to talk. This happened for three-and-a-half straight years. We would go over the batters and other strategy, like how to position players on the field. Stanley caught his first league game in 1947—after Goose got ticked at me.

See, it all started in the 1945 season when the Stars took part in an all-star round robin at Yankee Stadium.

It was us, the New York Black Yankees, an all-star team from North Carolina, and an all-star team from South Carolina. Our pay was based on the percentage of the gate. We had about fourteen thousand in the stands. And they gave every ballplayer just twenty-five dollars. Something wasn't right.

Now I wasn't trying to be difficult. I just wanted things to be fair, you know? When I went to get paid for that game, Eddie tried to hand me the twenty-five dollars.

"What's that for?"

"The game in Yankee Stadium," he said.

I said, "Look, Eddie, I majored in math when I was in school so I'm going to calculate for you. If there were just ten thousand in the stands, that comes out to seventy-nine dollars a man."

"Oh, that's what you say. Twenty-five dollars is what all the other guys got."

I looked at him funny and all but still took the money. But let me tell you, when I went to Venezuela for an all-star game in Maracaibo in 1946, my roommate was Marvin "Hack" Barker, manager of the New York Black Yankees. We were laying up in bed one night shooting the breeze, and he said to me, "Cash, you remember when you guys played in Yankee Stadium in that four-team, all-star game? You guys got twenty-five dollars a man, didn't you?"

"Yeah," I said.

"Know how much we got?"

"How much?"

"We got seventy-nine dollars a man."

Well, I just about fell out of my bed. I mean, that's what I had figured in front of Eddie Gottlieb. And guess what? I later found out that right after that game at Yankee Stadium, some guy named "Seck" barged into the room where Eddie and Bill Loshner, the promoters, were counting the game's receipts. Seck was the "front man" for the Black Yankees, and he caught Eddie and Bill skimming more than their share of money off the top, cheating the Stars players and Ed Bolden, the team's minority owner. So Seck blackmailed them and told them they'd better give him three thousand dollars or else he'd rat them out to Bolden. Needless to say, Seck got his money, and the Stars got screwed.

Then Goose started to get greedy too. When the Clowns, who were one of the biggest draws in the league, came to Shibe Park one night in 1947, Goose told his wife down in Memphis, Tennessee, to send a telegram that night saying their house burned down and everything in it was destroyed. Well, Goose knew that Clown game would bring in a lot of cash. We had about thirty-five thousand in the stands at $2.50 a person. After the game, Goose took the telegraph and some sad story in to Eddie and begged for three thousand dollars. Eddie handed him the cash.

I mean, come on now, Goose, how low can you go?

Anyway, by the end of the '47 season, I was really on Goose about this money thing. So how did he get me back? He benched me and let Stanley play. One day we went to Yankee Stadium for a doubleheader, and Goose was so mad at me that he sent me to the bullpen. Clarence "Spoon" Palm caught the first game.

We lost.

Stanley caught the second game.

We lost.

When we got back to Philly, Eddie Gottlieb called
Goose into his office and told him that whenever we
were in those big stadiums, Bill Cash, the first-string
catcher, was going to start. Well, you know Goose wasn't
happy to hear that. But I didn't care. I stayed on him
about his cheating us and about his shady dealings with
money.

Finally Goose went to Eddie's office and said, "Either
get rid of Cash or get rid of me."

Eddie got rid of Goose.

Oscar Charleston, the great outfielder who played
with Hilldale, the Homestead Grays, and Pittsburgh
Crawfords, took over as manager. See, I'm straight. I
don't believe in a whole lot of foolishness. And Goose
was into a bunch of foolishness when he should've been
just managing the team. If you respect me and the team,
then I'll respect you.

Winter came and it was time for me to head south. But
this time, I decided to play in Cuba. Over the years, Cuba
had become a favorite spot for both Negro Leaguers
and major leaguers. The island was simply beautiful.
It was easy to see why writer Ernest Hemingway loved
living there. It was simple to get to and had wonderful
weather, great baseball facilities. And right after the war,
Cuba was modernizing, so it was no longer some rinky-
dink country.

And, man, Cubans had a passion for baseball.
They'd been playing it down there since the 1870s, and
blacks had been going down there since around the
1900s. Many Cuban players made it to the majors before
African Americans did—at least officially. To hear some
tell it, several Cuban ballplayers had more than one
drop of black blood in them.

Josh, Cool, Satchel—all those guys played down in Cuba. There were some great players from there. I'm told pitcher Luis Tiant Sr., a native Cuban and father of the Boston Red Sox great Luis Jr., had a super pick-off move to first. In one game, Goose Curry was at the plate when Luis Sr. made his fancy move and threw to first. The move was so good that Goose swung and fell on his butt, thinking Luis had pitched the ball to him. That move must've been something else.

There was also a sense of freedom playing in Cuba and in other Latin American countries. In Cuba, you could be thirsty, and when you found a water fountain, you didn't have to worry that there was a "Whites Only" sign tacked over it. Shoot, the water even tasted better. I mean, you could go wherever, take your wife, and not be hassled because you were black. We Negro Leaguers were treated just like the white American ballplayers. And that sure felt good.

In Cuba, I played for two teams, Almendares from Havana for about two months, then Marianao on the outskirts of Havana. Now even though we black ballplayers could go just about anywhere we wanted, in Havana we were all booked in an old flea-bitten hotel. Well, I wasn't having none of that stuff. The other guys didn't care because being in Cuba was a chance for them to get away from their wives and girlfriends and do some "dissipating." So the condition of their rooms wasn't important—they had other things on their minds. But me? I had brought Sadie and Janet down with me while we left little Bill with relatives in South Miami to attend school. And when I went to sleep, I wanted to hold on to Sadie, not sink in the middle of a limp, bug-filled mattress.

So one day we checked out of that dump. Sadie and
I found a beautiful apartment near the ocean for $175
a month. When I got to the ballpark the next day, Mike
Guerrero, manager of Almendares, told me I'd been
traded to Marianao just because I moved out of the
hotel and got my own apartment.

But you know something? That was no problem. We
loved our new place right on the bay. I mean, every night
we fell asleep to the soothing sound of waves splashing
ashore. Our apartment was near Hotel Nacional,
a beautiful, luxurious place where movie stars like
George Raft and some Mafia types stayed and gambled
at its casino. The hotel, which history books described
as "Andalusian-Moorish style," had an impressive
background: Back in the 1930s, it was the refuge for
Cuban army officers trying to escape the wrath of some
upset soldiers whose leader was Fulgencio Batista. This
guy would later become Cuba's dictator. In fact, the
woman who rented us the apartment was one of Batista's
mistresses.

The only year I didn't go away for winter ball was
1948, and I really blew that. I was barnstorming with
the Indianapolis Clowns, that offbeat collection of
ballplayers that included comics like "King Tut" (Richard
King) and a midget named "Spec Bebop" (Ralph Bell).
And guess who was on the team with me? Jackie. Yep,
this was a year after he broke the color barrier with the
Brooklyn Dodgers.

Anyway, the Clowns made you laugh, but they could
play some serious ball. When the Clowns played, the
game was sometimes touted as a "combined baseball
and comedy show." This wasn't too surprising because
Abe Saperstein, the same guy who owned the Harlem

Globetrotters, owned the team. The Clowns put on routines like "Shadow Ball"—where the guys "fielded" and "threw" invisible balls. They pitched between their legs, staged funny skits on the sidelines. They even had the first woman to play pro ball, Tony Stone. The Clowns were the latest in a line of comedy baseball teams that knew entertaining people and playing baseball helped pay the bills—big time. Back in the day, there were the Zulu Cannibal Giants (now *they* were some crazy people. They wore grass skirts when they played. Buck O'Neil once played for them), the Florida Hobos, and the Ethiopian Clowns. But when it came time to be serious, the Clowns could play with the best of them.

In '48, the Clowns played their last game of the year in New Orleans. Jackie was playing second base, and I was catching. Now people talk about Jackie's temper and all, but I never saw it. He was always friendly, a nice guy to be around, even after all the crap he took in 1947. He may have been hotheaded around some other folks, but not around me.

Anyway, after that last game, Jackie asked me to go out west. He said, "Bill, come to California with me. We can make a lot of money playing in the winter leagues out there."

I said, "Nah. I'm going to go back to Philadelphia. Then I want to go away to play in the Latin countries." I really wanted to go back to Venezuela. So Jackie went to California without me.

As it turned out, I didn't go away at all. I got me a new job at home at Lester Piano Manufacturing Co.

You don't hear much about Lester pianos nowadays, but back then, they were considered among the best instruments in the world. For years, Lester Grands were used by the Philadelphia Orchestra and the Baltimore Symphony and played during presidential inaugurations. But it was the Spinet model created in the mid-1930s that really gave the company a boost. Spinets were smaller than the old uprights, but still had a great sound.

The company was started in the late 1800s in Center City Philadelphia, but moved and was named after the town it relocated to, Lester, Pennsylvania. Now this was no nickel-and-dime operation. The plant covered twelve acres, and at one time five hundred workers, tuners, cabinetmakers, and the like worked there. Eighty to one hundred pianos a day came out of that factory in the early 1950s.

My first job there was nothing to brag about. I pushed pianos from one room of the factory to another. It took four men to move the hefty instruments out of the "stringing" room and into the "squaring" room, where the piano backs were installed. We also made sure the backs fit square on the piano before it was moved to its next destination. It was a makeshift assembly line. We put about seventy backs on a day. And you know something? In those days, a piano was tuned nine times before it was shipped out. And all but one of the men who did the tuning while I was there was blind.

At Lester, I didn't have a chance to use my mechanical skills like I did at Sun Ship, but the job offered some flexibility. I never worked longer than two-and-a-half months straight. Every summer, the plant shut down seven weeks for inventory.

One year during this down time, I decided to drive for the Yellow Cab Co. I knew my way around the city pretty well, and the hours 6 p.m. to 3 a.m. weren't bad.

The one thing I quickly learned was to stay away from the most popular taxi pickup places. People swarmed the Reading Terminal in downtown Philadelphia, but if you got into that cab line, you could be there a long time before that blue light outside the terminal flashed, a signal for the next cab to pull in and pick up a fare. I liked roaming the streets. I got more turnovers that way and more money.

But I didn't want to spend my life as a hack. I put in for jobs at the Boeing plant and New York Shipbuilding but didn't get one at either place. I wound up back at the piano company.

One day in 1948, I was walking past the Bartram High School field, where a baseball game was being played. You know I loved baseball, no matter who was playing, and I really liked games that involved kids. So I walked over for a closer look. It was Gratz High School versus Bartram. And Bartram's coach looked familiar to me. Darn if it wasn't Mr. Kistenmacher, my old baseball coach from Overbrook who started a less-talented Jewish guy ahead of me.

"Cash, I've been following you in the newspapers," Kistenmacher said, like a proud father talking to his son. "You're doing good work."

"Thanks," I said but kept my real thoughts to myself. *I told you I was good. That'll teach you not to be prejudiced.*

So what did my real dad think about my success? Well, yeah, he had followed my career, but he didn't cut out any stories from the newspapers and save them in a scrapbook like some parents might've done. Mom didn't know much about the game but was proud of my success. I remember one time she came to a Liberty Stars game. The other team was up and got a hit. And Mom started cheering up a storm, until one of my teammates explained to her she was rooting against her son.

The East-West All-Star games were the highlight of the Negro League season, even more prestigious than winning the championship. These games, started in 1933, were the brainchild of either Crawford owner Gus Greenlee or Crawford secretary Roy Sparrow. The games were big moneymakers that brought excitement and glamour to the league and its players. The game was played in Chicago's old Comiskey Park and drew as many as fifty thousand people, black and white.

According to some history books, that first game featured—now get this—Cool, Josh, catcher Biz Mackey of the Philadelphia Stars, outfielder Oscar Charleston, and third baseman Judy Johnson, both of the Pittsburgh Crawfords, on the East squad. Shortstop Willie Wells, who was named to the Hall of Fame, and first baseman Mule Suttles, both of the Chicago American Giants, and right fielder Sam Bankhead of the Nashville Elite Giants were among those who played for the West. I mean, these players are legends.

So when I got selected to the East team in 1948 and 1949, I was on Cloud 9. The 1948 East team had players like Buck Leonard of the Homestead Grays, Monte Irvin of the Newark Eagles, Orestes Minoso of the New York Cubans—man, that guy could play some third base—and my teammate Frank Austin. That year the West had Quincy Trouppe of the Chicago American Giants, Robert Boyd of the Memphis Red Sox, and Art Wilson of the Birmingham Black Barons. We were shut out 3-0 in front of forty-two thousand people on August 22. I was one of two catchers on the East team; Louis

Louden of the New York Cubans was the other. I didn't play in that game.

Two days later, we had another East-West game called "The Dream Game." Held in Yankee Stadium, this was part of the league's effort to bring the popular all-star game to the eastern part of the country. This was only the third year they tried it, and it didn't have the same excitement as the real deal in Chicago—in fact, only eighteen thousand fans showed up. And to be honest, I don't remember much about it. But according to stats found in Larry Lester's book *Black Baseball's National Showcase,* I went one for three and scored a run. The East won 6-1.

In the 1949 game, we shut out the West 4-0 in one of the most satisfying games of my career.

This is what happened. The East went in as four-to-one underdogs. Man, we had to face the likes of the Monarchs' power hitting Willard Brown, who led his division with eighteen home runs in 1948, and Birmingham Black Barons' infielder Lorenzo "Piper" Davis, who finished the season batting a hefty .378. Plus most of the West's pitchers, as usual, came from the strong Monarch staff: Gene Richardson and Jim "Lefty" LaMarque. There was also Gready "Lefty" McKinnis from the Chicago American Giants and Willie "Ace" Hutchinson of the Memphis Red Sox.

There was a reported thirty-one thousand people in Comiskey Park's stands (I think there were really twice that many), and Happy Chandler, commissioner of baseball, had the pleasure of sitting in my box in the stands with Sadie.

Sure enough, I started. I cracked a double in one of my four times at the plate. No one stole a base on me. I was playing so well that Hack Barber, who was supposed to catch six innings of the game, told me to stay in. My Stars teammate Bob Griffith not only got the win but also drove in a run. And the big gun for us that game was Howard Easterling, third baseman for the New York Cubans, who went two for four and drove in a run.

The Stars had a mediocre year in 1949. The first half of the season we went 13-20; good enough for third place in a five-team division. The first-place Baltimore Elite Giants' record was 24-12. I couldn't tell you our record in the second half, but it didn't matter—the Giants were division champs.

That year, we made a road trip I'll never forget. We played the Clowns in Indianapolis on a Thursday and had to be in Tyler, Texas, to play the Houston Eagles by Saturday. The Eagles used to be in Newark, New Jersey, and I sure wish they'd kept their butts there because it would've made things a lot easier travel-wise.

We only got four hours of sleep before we loaded up the bus and started south. The back of the bus was stuffed with bags and our uniforms. Four ballplayers doubled as drivers. I drove from 2 to 7 a.m., and we had to haul butt to cover nearly nine hundred miles in three days. It felt like two thousand miles. And remember, the highway system wasn't as good as it is now, so the driving wasn't always smooth. By the time we pulled into Tyler, we were whupped.

And then the ignorance started.

First we weren't allowed to change into our uniforms in the stadium club house or use its showers. Now here we were in a city named after the tenth president of the United States, John Tyler, and we were being treated like foreigners. We changed at the YMCA. Then while we were out on the field, this guy in the stands started yelling, "Hey, nigger. I'm gonna shoot you! Nigger, I'm gonna shoot you!" You might find this hard to believe, but usually when the Stars played, we didn't encounter racism on the field or from the stands. But this day, after a long hot bus ride to this city ninety-five miles east of Dallas, here was this cracker threatening us.

Even if I weren't so tired, I probably wouldn't have gone over to him and said anything. I mean, we heard the curses so often off the field that the words just washed over us. We learned to keep quiet and do what we had to do. It went in one ear and out the other. Besides, it was 105 degrees at 7 p.m. in Tyler, and we weren't about to expend a whole lot of energy on this foolishness. I was confident there'd be no shooting, not with all the cops stationed around the field. We had a game to play—which we promptly lost 9-2.

All during the '49 season, I got nibbles from the majors. The Dodgers had me scouted. It was so serious that one day, when we went to play the Bushwicks in New York, the guys were congratulating me and said they heard I was going to Montreal, home of the Dodgers' Triple A team, where Jackie prepared for the majors.

I was excited as all get out. I asked Eddie Gottlieb if he had heard from anybody from the Dodger organization, and he said no. Then I got the word from some other scouts, who said, "Bill, the price doubled on you." That greedy Gottlieb had priced me out of the Dodgers' range. Same thing happened when we went to Indianapolis for a two-game set with the Clowns. A scout from the Milwaukee Braves was in town to look me over. I played first base on Friday night then caught

Saturday night's game, which we won 1-0. After the game, Charleston, our manager, told me I was going to the Braves organization. Well, after what happened back in New York, I kept my excitement in check.

And a good thing I did. Fred Banks, who owned a semi-pro team and worked as a scout for major league teams, broke the news to me: Gottlieb had doubled the price on me. Again. "You're the backbone of the team," Fred said to me. Well, I always thought Gene Benson was the Stars' backbone. And I couldn't take any solace in Fred's words. Greed was ruining my chances to make the majors.

By the end of the season, I was still a Star. But after watching Gottlieb in action, I became a much smarter Star. If Gottlieb was going to benefit financially from selling my rights, I was going to benefit too. So we worked out a deal: Whatever price he got for me, I'd get 30 percent.

Man, I couldn't wait to return to Caracas to play winter ball. The pay in Latin countries was good: one thousand dollars a month plus expenses—and the weather was great. And I figured out how to make my stay down there more enjoyable: between practices and games, I went to school to learn Spanish.

Occasionally I'd bring Sadie and the kids down to visit. After all, I spent five months away from them living in a hotel in a strange land, so having my family around, even for just a little while, was important. Sadie had opened a beauty shop in Philadelphia, but she'd close it, send her customers to another cosmetologist, and come live with me. Sadie said we were treated like royalty in Latin America, and there didn't seem to be any racism.

But there was one thing down there she hated: those nasty lizards. Man, they made themselves just as much at home in our apartment as we did.

Anyway, I stayed in Caracas for only part of the '49 winter season because Sadie and I had decided to buy a house in Philadelphia, and I returned to help take care of business back home. Shoot, it was about time we moved too. We had lived in my parents' house at 7920 Brewster Avenue for nine years. My folks even let Sadie set up her first beauty shop on the front porch. But now I was making enough money for us to buy our own place. We had our eyes on a house behind 7920 Brewster, which was owned by a retiree. And when he decided to finally sell, we jumped on it.

We moved into 7915 Botanic Avenue, a house that became very special to us. It was the only house on the block with a white picket fence. It also had a huge side yard where Sadie planted roses and other pretty plants and flowers. Man, we loved that house.

There was no way we were going to leave Elmwood. We'd grown close to our neighbors. We enjoyed the neighborhood traditions, like going to the ball games and socializing with friends. By that time, the neighborhood team was Tinicum AC, not the old Liberty Stars that I once played for, and they had games at Eighty-eighth and Tinicum Avenue.

Let me tell you a little about Elmwood. It was the most integrated neighborhood in Philadelphia. And living there taught me something: that you don't judge a person by the color of his skin. There were so many different ethnic groups, races, and religions living in that pocket of Philadelphia. Everyone looked out for one another. Even though I may have been away playing ball much of the time, Bill Jr. knew he couldn't get into too much nonsense, like taking a swim in Cobbs Creek, because Elmwood eyes were watching. The neighbors would let Sadie know what happened before Bill Jr. even got home.

We had some white neighbors, the Rybacks, who kept an eye on our house. If a stranger came to our door and we weren't in, the Rybacks were quickly on the case. "What do you want?" they'd demand of the intruder. We thought the place was paradise.

I was in great shape when spring training rolled around in 1950, but our league was in bad shape. With the majors finally picking up Negro League ballplayers, teams like the Monarchs, the Clowns, and even the Stars saw attendance dip. Now, no matter what day of the week, our fans could go to big league parks and see their colored heroes play with the white boys of organized ball. Negro League players were becoming legitimate in the eyes of white America, but our acceptance by white America meant the Negro Leagues were dying.

The Stars' spring training that year was in Charleston, South Carolina, where we had beautiful weather, eighty-five degrees every day and low humidity. Funny, now spring training lasts for weeks. But back then we took just eight days to get ready for the season. Anyway, we got in good shape. I did a lot of running because I believe no athlete is better than his legs. The guys would yell at me, "Bill! It's your time to hit." But I didn't care nothing about batting practice. I just wanted to run.

We started the exhibition season in Jacksonville, Florida, where we played the Jacksonville Red Caps, then came up southern Virginia, playing teams along the way, making our way back north.

Opening day finally arrived. It was a Sunday, and we were at the Memorial Stadium in Baltimore to play the Elite Giants. Right before the game began, Bus Clarkson, our shortstop and team captain, moseyed up to me with two telegrams, one for him and one for me.

"Ernesto Carmona, the manager of the Mexico City Red Devils, is gonna be in town," Bus said to me. "They need a catcher and a shortstop to go to Mexico City."

"You going?"

"Heck, yeah, I'm going," Bus said. "After we get back to Philadelphia tonight, he's going to be at my house around nine."

So that night, I went to Bus' house. After he introduced me to Carmona, Bus and his wife went upstairs. I thought that was a little strange since we were both talking about playing for Carmona, but I didn't worry much about it. I asked Carmona about all of the major league players they had in Mexico, because 1949 was the last year they were allowed to play in that league. The major leagues, seeing so much talent drift south, signed an agreement with the Caribbean teams that regulated player movement. But still, they were getting great money. I heard Max Lanier of the St. Louis Browns went down there and supposedly made thirty-five thousand dollars a year.

Anyway, after a little small talk, Carmona, in a thick accent, said, "We'd like to have you."

"Well, what are you paying? You paid a major league left-hander thirty-five thousand dollars and the most games he ever won was thirteen. I want some of that money. I want twenty-five thousand."

So Carmona got to stuttering. "Oh, no, no, no. We got rid of the major leaguers. We don't pay that kind of money no more."

"So what are you paying?"

"We'll pay five hundred dollars a month."

I'm thinking, is this guy serious? I mean, I was making five hundred dollars a month with the Stars. And when I played in Cuba or Venezuela, I pulled in one thousand dollars a month plus expenses. And he wanted me to leave my family to play in Mexico for a lousy five hundred dollars a month?

"Look," I said, "we have a doubleheader at Shibe Park tomorrow night. Come on out. If you like what you see, OK. If you don't, it's all right with me."

So he asked me to name my price.

"I'll come for one thousand dollars, plus expenses and a round-trip ticket. And I want one thousand up front before I leave." See, that's something Josh Gibson taught us about negotiating. He'd say whenever you go to the Latin countries, always get a month's pay up front because things are going to be different down there. It takes a while to adapt to the altitude, and chances are you won't be playing your best the first few days. With the up-front money, the owners down there will be more patient with you. Shoot, they're businessmen, and they want to get their money's worth.

"We're not going to pay that kind of money down there," Carmona said.

"I'm gonna catch one of those games tomorrow night. You might like what you see."

Shibe Park was packed. Anytime the Indianapolis Clowns were in town, you were guaranteed two things:

big crowds and a good game. That night the Clowns had this kid named Raul Galata on the mound. He was a strong left-hander who didn't know the word quit. The Clowns had him pitch both games. And you know what? That kid threw eighteen straight zeros at us and shut us out both games.

In the game I played in, I handled our ace right-hander, Bill Ricks, and we gave those Clowns a run for their money. Galata gave up only four hits that game, and I got two of them. I shot down two guys trying to steal second and picked another one off first base. We lost 1-0, but it was one of the best games I ever caught. I knew it was a good game because that old hurting in the back of my head returned, the hurting I got when I concentrated so hard, remembering what pitches batters liked, what they hit last time up, where to position the fielders—those kinds of things.

About 1:30 a.m., the phone rang at my house. Sadie was miffed, wondering who in the world would call at such an hour. I picked up the receiver, ready to lay out whoever thought we'd want to have a conversation at that hour.

"Boy, you're good." It was Carmona. He had the team owner send me the one thousand dollars up-front money and the round-trip tickets. Friday night, I left for Mexico City. My career as a Star was over.

CHAPTER 9

A LUKEWARM WELCOME
AND RED-HOT LIE

✳ ✳ ✳

I remember one game I got five hits and stole five bases,
but none of it was written down because they forgot to
bring the scorebook to the game that day.
                                        —James "Cool Papa" Bell

That flight from Philadelphia to Mexico was the longest journey of my life. I was anxious, and the time zone changes and feeling of uncertainty didn't help none. We left Philly at 10 p.m. on one of those DC-4s. We landed in Dallas about 2 a.m. to refuel before flying to Mexico City.

By the time we got to Mexico City, it was 8 a.m., and we still had to go through customs. Man, I was tired as all get out. All the way down, I had to sit next to one of the plane's engines, and its rumbling kept me awake. I had carried my equipment and uniform with me so I wouldn't have to rush to the field to change. I had to be at the ballpark by noon.

Finally we got to the hotel, and I thought I'd get a chance to catch some sleep. Well, I hadn't been in bed more than thirty minutes before Carmona called. It was 9:30.

"Boy, are you all right? Are you all right?"

I told him I was fine, hung up, turned over in my bed, and tried to go to sleep. The phone rang at 10 a.m. It was Carmona. He wanted to know if I was OK.

"Look, don't call me no more. I gotta be on the field in two hours."

Carmona called me at 10:30. Then at 11:00. Then at 11:30.

I finally got up and struggled into my uniform. Talk about tired! Carmona had been in the hotel lobby the last time he called—shoot, he may have been there all morning for all I knew. He got us a cab, and we went to the ballpark.

Let me tell you, there were thirty-five thousand Mexicans in the stands. In Mexico, baseball was almost a religion. It was played three times a week, once on Saturday afternoon and twice on Sundays. The Sunday games were special. In the heavily Catholic country, fans got up early, attended 7 a.m. Mass, then went to the ballpark, where they spent the rest of the day. There was usually a 9 a.m. game and one in the afternoon.

Mexicans played baseball nearly year-round. You can thank the Cubans for bringing baseball to Mexico. I'm told that in the 1890s, Cubans fleeing their country during one of their revolutions came west to Mexico, bringing their love for the sport with them.

On this Saturday, the fans were revved up by newspaper and television reports of my coming to play for the Red Devils. Heck, I didn't know my arrival had caused such a stir.

I knew a couple of the ballplayers on my team. There was Burnis "Bill" Wright, a power-hitting outfielder for the Baltimore Elite Giants, who, historians say, batted around .300 most of his twenty-five years in baseball. And there was first baseman Lorenzo "Chiquitin" Cabrera, who played with the New York Cubans and played with me in Cuba and the Dominican Republic. He would enjoy his greatest season as a ballplayer that year, hitting .354.

"You look to be my fourth-place hitter," Carmona said, looking me over before the game.

"I can't play," I said. "I'm too tired. What about Bill Wright? He's the usual cleanup hitter."

"No. You gotta play. Everybody knows you're here. You've been on the news, all over television and radio. You gotta play."

So I played. And we lost. I went an embarrassing 0 for 5. Not quite the impression I wanted to make my first day in Mexico. And, man, I heard about it. The next day, I was being called the "*Grand Paquete*" in the press. I knew a little Spanish, but didn't know what "*Grand Paquete*" meant. Bill Wright translated it for me: "Big Package." The sportswriters and broadcasters were basically saying I was being paid a lot of money but was mediocre.

That hurt. I couldn't blame them, though. I played lousy. Like I said, I was tired, traveling all the way from Philadelphia then not being able to get any sleep—thanks to that crazy Carmona calling me every thirty minutes. Well, being called "*Grand Paquete*" did two things for me. It showed me how passionate the Mexicans were about baseball, and it made me determined to show Mexico City that Bill "Ready" Cash was no deadbeat ballplayer.

Sunday morning, I was ready. I had eaten a good dinner and got a good night's sleep, so I was rejuvenated. We went up against Monterey. Our pitcher was a guy named Warren, who I believe was the only white pitcher in the Mexican League that year. I had played against him in Venezuela in '49, so I was a little familiar with his stuff. Monterey's manager was a guy named Salazar, who was my manager in Caracas.

Just like the night before, I batted cleanup. My first trip to the plate, I stroked a double between third and the line. Next time up, I shot a single over shortstop. On my third at bat, I sliced a single over the second baseman's head and later hit another double down the third base line. All in all, I went four for five and the fans went crazy. And you know something? I never heard the phrase "*Grand Paquete*" ever again.

Mexico soon became one of my favorite countries. The competition was stiff. How stiff? Well, Roy Campanella, who made it to the Dodgers, was only the tenth best catcher ever to play in Mexico, according to a newspaper article. I was ranked the fourth best. The atmosphere was good, and the people were real, real nice. Plus it was cheap to live there. Shoot, you could live anywhere in Mexico City for three pesos. And I was making good money down there, which really helped things back in Philly. We had just bought the house, but we couldn't afford the furniture we wanted. We only had a kitchen set. When I got paid in Mexico, I sent the money home, and we bought furniture for the parlor and dining room.

I remember I shared an apartment with pitchers Rufus Lewis and Robert Griffith. Rufus, who played with the Newark/Houston Eagles, shared a bedroom with me. Robert, a teammate of mine from Philadelphia, had the master bedroom all to himself. Bill Wright had an apartment downstairs. We were doing so well that we paid a maid one hundred pesos a month to cook breakfast, clean the apartment, and wash our clothes. That was a good forty pesos more than maids normally got. But she still tried to screw us over. After a while, she wanted extra money to wash our clothes, even though we agreed from the start those chores were part of her job. We got rid of her butt.

Our new maid took full advantage of our hospitality. We told her to help herself to anything in the apartment. Why'd we go and do that? One day while we were away at practice, she helped herself to the beer and rum we kept on hand for guests. When we returned home after practice, we found the door locked from the inside. We knocked and knocked, but no answer. Finally the team shortstop crawled through a window and let us in. And you know what? There was our maid, sprawled out drunk as a skunk on Griffith's bed. We got rid of her too.

Bill and Robert Griffith share a laugh in Mexico City in 1950. (Credit: From the personal collection of Bill "Ready" Cash.)

Anyway, I learned an important lesson playing baseball in Mexico: you couldn't beat the Latin ballplayers by throwing heat past them. You had to finesse them. Satchel played in Mexico in the late 1930s, and even he found out that Latin players were fastball hitters. They teed off on Satch's hard stuff, which wasn't good, considering Satch was reportedly getting about two thousand dollars a month. A sore arm forced him to rely on his looping curveball to cut the corners of the plate. I used to tell my pitchers to throw Latin batters two really bad curveballs then bust them with a fastball. You have to set those guys up, make them think.

But I remember one game where setting up a Latin batter almost cost a Mexico City teammate his life.

We were leading Veracruz 2-1. They had a man on second, and Lorenzo Cabrera's power-hitting brother, whose name escapes me right now, came up to bat. I told Rufus Lewis to throw him inside and tight, you know, brush him back off the plate.

Well, the batter didn't take too kindly to the first pitch. He stepped back and slammed home plate with his bat. I didn't pay him no mind and signaled Rufus to throw a breaking curveball. He delivered. Unfortunately the curve broke right into the batter's ribs. So as I chased down the ball, the batter sprinted out to the mound, bat in hand. He reared it back and cracked Rufus in the back of the head. Rufus crumbled on the mound.

Just as the batter was about to unleash another blow, Bill Wright appeared out of nowhere with a bat and smashed him across the forehead, splitting his head open. Man, it was nasty, but years afterward Rufus would say Bill saved his life.

I truly believe it was fate, along with the greed of Stars' owner Eddie Gottlieb, that brought me to Mexico. It turned out that offer to play in Mexico was part of a bigger plan—I'd like to say conspiracy—to sell me to the highest bidder, just as the Negro Leagues were going down the tubes.

Remember, right before the 1950 season, Eddie got calls from at least three major league teams wanting me: the Dodgers, the Braves, and the Giants. But he figured that the asking price on my talents would increase, and he'd rake in more money. So he held on to my rights. But the Braves also wanted Bus Clarkson, our shortstop, and Stanley Glenn. See, Bus never did go to Mexico with me and Carmona. The Braves signed him and Stanley.

So even though I was playing in Mexico, I was still the property of the Philadelphia Stars. But in all honesty, the Stars were the farthest thing from my mind.

When I arrived in Mexico, the Red Devils were seventh in an eight-team league. Every time Carmona needed some baseball strategy, he turned to me. And it worked. We started winning. The season came down to the last series. We were facing Guadalajara, with whom we were tied for first.

It had been a pretty exciting week leading up to this game. I had gone to a bullring to watch my first bullfight. They were filming a scene for a movie; I think it was *The Magnificent Matador,* starring Anthony Quinn and Maureen O'Hara. Quinn played a matador who suddenly turned chicken after teaching his protégé nearly all the bullfighting ropes. They made a big deal about it. Posters were everywhere, encouraging folks to be extras, get a free lunch and a chance to see Quinn and two of the country's best bullfighters, Antonio Ordonez and Carlos Aruza, who were film consultants.

In one bullfight scene, a bullfighter made a mistake and got gored. Well, he had some guts because he came right back and asked to fight the bull again, this time with just a red handkerchief—and on his knees. When the horn blew, which signaled he had lasted the required time, he got one of those long sword things and plunged it into the bull, stopping it dead in its tracks. The crowd roared, and one girl sitting in front of us was so impressed she threw her pocketbook into the bullring. Man, it was pretty exciting.

The day of the big game in Guadalajara was sunny as usual and there were about nine thousand five hundred packed in the stadium. We were leading 6-0 in the third when Guadalajara's little shortstop came up to bat. Carmona wanted to walk him, which would've loaded the bases.

I said to Carmona, "You don't want to walk him. We got the lead. That wouldn't make sense."

"You walk him," he said. "I'm the manager."

"I don't play to lose," I said. "When I put on that uniform, I play to win."

While we argued, I could hear our fans screaming, "No, Cash! No, Cash!" See, unlike Carmona, they knew their baseball. They didn't want us to walk this guy, either. But Carmona kept insisting we put this guy on base. Well, I just got frustrated. Here was this manager who had been following my advice all year, and suddenly he turned stupid on me. No, I wasn't going to walk the guy. Carmona had had enough. He told me to take off my equipment and get off the field.

I stormed into the dugout, madder than all get out. A few seconds later, a few of my Red Devil teammates came in after me. "Come on, Bill, we need you," they said. So I went back out onto the field, and against all my baseball instincts, I had the pitcher walk the shortstop.

Well, you can guess what happened. The next batter, a young Cuban named Arnesaba, slammed the ball to right center, right into the mouth of a man painted on an outfield billboard smoking a Camel cigarette. The grand slam made it 6-4. We tied it two innings later, but in the eighth, they got two more runs, making it 8-6.

In the ninth, we squeezed across three runs to take the lead 9-8. We were on the verge of pulling the game out and becoming league champions. Then the rains came. They were hard, fast, heavy rains. I swear, the field was under four inches of water in almost ten minutes. We couldn't finish playing, and according to league rules, the game ended with the score of the last complete inning. That was the eighth, when Guadalajara led 8-6.

So Guadalajara was the champ, but we could've been the champs if Carmona wasn't so darn hardheaded. In sixty-two games that year, I hit .310 with thirty-nine runs batted in (RBIs). And I made a lot of money. Sadie and I bought more furniture for the house. But to this day, I still have an empty feeling. We had a chance to win a championship, my first ever, and we missed it.

When I returned to Philly, I planned to go back to work at the Lester Piano Company and spend time with the family. But shortly after I settled into our new house, I got a call to return to Mexico. A team called Culiacan in the Mexican Pacific Coast League needed a catcher. Even though I was thirty-one, I was still in excellent shape and considered myself to be in my prime. Shoot,

Satchel played ball till he was in his sixties or something like that.

I had no problem returning to Mexico for the winter. The Red Devils didn't want me back. I don't know why, but it was just as well because it was hard playing for a stubborn and insecure manager like Carmona.

Anyway, on my trip to Culiacan, I realized I still had a lot to learn about traveling and racism. I flew into Tucson, Arizona, on December 15, 1950, and took a cab to Nogales, a city that straddled the Mexico/Arizona border. From there, I was to fly into Culiacan, about six hundred miles northwest of Mexico City. I had a choice of staying either on the Mexican side or the American side of Nogales. I picked the American side because I thought things there would be like they were in Laredo, Texas. Let me explain: Laredo, Texas, which also is on the Mexico/U.S. border, had a sister city, Nuevo Laredo in Mexico, right across the Rio Grande River. When Negro League ballplayers played in Mexico close to Laredo, Texas, we often crossed the border to eat because there was a cook there who could whip up some mean "home food," a tasty break from that Mexican stuff we were eating all the time. And in Lardeo, Texas, there wasn't no discrimination. So I thought things would be the same way on the American side of Nogales. By that time, black ballplayers were gaining ground in America. Jackie, Larry, and a handful of other Negro Leaguers had crossed the barrier. Things were looking up.

Well, I got to Nogales around 11 a.m., missing by three hours the plane that flew out once a day into Mexico. So I checked into a hotel and went to bed. Around 6 p.m., I woke up hungry as all get out and went to a restaurant to have dinner.

"I'm sorry, sir," the waiter said to me. "I can't serve you here."

You know why they wouldn't serve me. It was because I was a Negro. I didn't start no fuss. I got a cabbie to pick me up a sandwich, which I ate in my room. That was my dinner—a sandwich. It was humiliating. Negro Leaguers may have been getting into the majors, but the people in Nogales didn't let me forget that I was a black man in white America. Every year after that, when I went to Nogales, I always stayed on the Mexican side, where they had a nine-story hotel called the Fray Marcos de Niza, and everybody in that hotel knew us ballplayers. The minute I got to customs, people were calling my name and asking for baseballs, so I always kept a fresh ball on top of my traveling bag.

The Culiacan team was much better than the Red Devils. My new teammates were more professional—you know I'm stickler for that—and more united. And playing for Culiacan was different too. We played in Mexico City two weeks then hit the road for two weeks. We wound up in towns such as Nuevo Laredo, San Luis Potosi, Torreon, and Monterrey. Usually we traveled by train, but when we went to Veracruz, we took the bus.

Now let me tell you a little something about Mexican tequila. I'm no drinker, but that stuff did wonders—when it came to fighting a cold. Here's my secret: a nice hot shower, a double shot of tequila with lemon, get under the bed covers, and boom—the next thing you know, you wake up cold-free. Natives of that country were used to the potent brew. I remember sometimes when a few got a load under their belts they'd stand up and scream, "*Recuerdo el* Alamo! *Recuerdo el* Alamo!" That's "Remember the Alamo," the battle cry associated with Texans who sought independence from Mexico back in 1835. The battle at the San Antonio mission happened in 1836, when Mexican forces stormed the place and beat Jim Bowie, Davy Crockett, and those guys. I guess the Mexicans were proud they had beaten them.

I set a bunch of records in the Pacific Coast League. While in Mexico, I learned Eddie Gottlieb decided my stock was as high as it would get, and he sold my rights to the Granby Braves of the Provincial League for ten thousand dollars. And thanks to my own wheeling and dealing, I got three thousand dollars of that.

Granby is in Canada, about fifty miles east of Montreal. Just like during the days of the Underground Railroad, when Canada was the goal for runaway slaves, the country became a haven for Negro League players too. The Canadian people loved the black ballplayers and black musicians, who also found a comfortable home there. And it wasn't a patronizing sort of appreciation, either.

The guy who owned the Pepsi-Cola factory in Granby also owned the ball club. My contract with the Braves paid me one hundred dollars, plus six hundred dollars under the table. Not bad.

The Braves had a few Negro Leaguers on the roster. A couple of old teammates, pitchers Bill Ricks and Roy Partlow, were with us. There was infielder Alfred "Buddy" Armour, pitcher Bob "School Boy" Griffith, and Joe Montero. Now Montero was actually Indian, but in our eyes, he was as black as us.

The six of us stayed in a big house owned by Ramone Forand and his wife. Forand was "the law" in Granby, and he took us in like we were family. The Forands' house had three extra bedrooms, so we slept two to a room. His wife cooked and washed our dirty clothes—everything. Guess how much we paid for all of this? Just six dollars a week!

The Provincial League that year had six teams and played a 126-game season. Some Negro League and major league teams liked to send players there for conditioning. Besides Granby (Philadelphia Stars), there were Three Rivers (Boston Braves), St. Jean (New York Black Yankees), Farnham (Homestead Grays), Sherbrooke (New York Cubans), and Drummondville (Newark Eagles). The team from Three Rivers was lousy. The Braves were sending up Class C players, and they were getting their butts kicked. Farnham, coached by the great Sam Bankhead, was also weak.

So we thought.

We went into the season's final game with Farnham, tied for first place with Sherbrooke. But Farnham brought in Grays pitcher Robert "Bill" Trice, who shut us out 1-0. I got two hits that game, but so what? We lost by a percentage point to Sherbrooke, with Drummondville coming in third. Trice, by the way, went to play for the Philadelphia Athletics.

I really liked Canada and did well with Granby. I finished the year hitting .310 (although the record books say I hit .296), with sixteen home runs, my all-time high, and fifty-four RBIs, another high. I was named the league's all-star catcher. I began to get offers from other Canadian teams, including Toronto, but I stayed with Granby.

Ramone, whose son was our batboy, had a lot to do with me staying there. Ramone loved us Negro League players. If we had an off day, he'd fill up his car's gas

tank and give us the keys. Didn't matter to him where we
might go (although it was usually to Montreal, about an
hour away). His only worry was that we might refill the
tank once we returned. He didn't want us doing that.
And Mrs. Forand treated us so nicely. After the season, I
got the boys together, and we pitched in fifteen dollars
apiece to buy her a fancy Elgin watch. We had it engraved
"From the Boys." Man, she was so proud of that watch.
Years later, the Forands would come to Atlantic City on
vacation. They were sure to look us up, and Mrs. Forand
was sure to be wearing that watch.

One time we met with a little trouble in Canada. I
was out with Bill Ricks when we ran into this cracker.
He called Bill a nigger. Well, I had known Bill most of
his baseball life, and I knew he wasn't somebody to mess
with. He was quick to reach for his blade. Sure enough,
Bill went for his knife and started after the man. I
grabbed him and held him back.

"Don't do it, roomie!"

A few minutes later, Mr. Forand, who was the town's
police chief and fire chief, arrived and grabbed the
cracker by the collar. "These are my boys," Forand said.
"And if you bother 'em, I'll lock you up and throw away
the key."

You might think I would've had more run-ins like
that playing baseball. But truth be told, those incidents
were rare. Yeah, there was that woman on the plane and
a tense situation in Tyler, Texas. But overall, not as many
problems as you might expect.

For the most part, the white fans respected us. When
they came to watch us play, it was out of curiosity that
grew into respect. They knew we had great players.
Every once in a while you got a white knucklehead who

shouted names at you. But my response was just go out and play ball. I mean, I heard the words—nigger, coon, jungle bunny—but in a way, I didn't hear them. Their evilness was lost in the ballpark winds. Shoot, I had a game to play.

Same thing with the white players. Some showed off when Jackie hit the majors, but those who gave him a hard time hadn't played with us in barnstorming games or in the Latin countries. Most were narrow-minded, insecure little boys trying to find their manhood by screaming curses and making threats.

Like that crude little Southern cracker Ben Chapman, the manager of the Phillies back in '47. When the Phillies came to Ebbets Field for a three-game series with the Dodgers, Jackie caught holy hell from the Phillies dugout, lead by that gutter-mouth Chapman. Jackie said he almost broke down because of that stuff.

But you know, I have to give Pee Wee Reese and some of the other Dodgers credit. In his book *I Never Had It Made,* Jackie says the Phillies were yelling things like, "Hey, nigger, why don't you go back to the cotton field where you belong?" and "Hey, snowflake, which one of those white boys' wives are you dating tonight?" (I'm sure they didn't use the word "dating.") But some of Jackie's teammates shouted back, "Listen, you yellow-bellied cowards, why don't you yell at someone who can answer back?" Pee Wee was always a big supporter of Jackie's. I always loved him for that. For the most part, the prejudice wasn't in the players. It was in the team owners.

By the end of 1951, I was itching to play major league ball. Jackie and Larry Doby in the American League had opened the door, and I was eager to step in. But integration had a devastating downside: It killed the Negro Leagues.

The new Negro National League, which the Stars belonged to, dissolved after the 1948 season. The Stars, New York Cubans, and Baltimore Elite Giants joined Indianapolis and Louisville in the eastern division of the still viable Negro American League. By 1950, the real East-West All-Star game was over. The Stars' final season was 1951. And by 1953, only four cities had teams calling themselves the Negro Leagues: Kansas City, Birmingham, Indianapolis, and Memphis.

By 1955, the league was gone, replaced by a few barnstorming teams.

See, once the major league teams started accepting black players, the Negro Leagues lost its special quality. Negro Leaguers were attracted to the majors, not so much because of money—heck, Satchel took a pay cut to pitch for Cleveland in 1948—but for the recognition and acceptance. To be able to say, "Hey, I made it," that we had got to a place closed to us for so long. We knew we were as good as players in "organized" ball, and we wanted to show it.

The major league owners played along. It wasn't out of the goodness of their hearts that they decided to let blacks in. It was the desire to win and make money.

To me, it wasn't about the money. It was about pride, about putting my skills on display for the whole nation to see. When the Chicago White Sox bought out my contract in 1952, I thought I was on my way.

I spent part of 1952 in Mexico, playing right field for Culiacan. We had a terrible year, losing twelve in a row. I was playing well, but still got my release and was signed by the Chicago White Sox organization. That was OK by me. The White Sox said I topped their list of catching prospects.

They sent me a contract for $325 a month. That was a little insulting, considering I was making $675 in Mexico and $750 in Canada. OK, so six hundred dollars of that Canadian money was paid under the table. But still, how was I going to support Sadie and the kids and pay bills on $325 a month?

Sadie and I talked it over. Yeah, I said, the White Sox money was piddling. But I could go to Victoria, Texas, for spring training—they had already sent me a ticket—and show how good I was. This could be my ticket into the majors. The White Sox wanted me for their Colorado Springs farm team, which was in the Western League. And it wasn't unusual for players in the Western League to jump into the majors.

We had a few dollars in the bank that Sadie could use while waiting for me to send more from Victoria.

Sadie was hurt that I was going away and she again would be responsible for raising the kids. But she knew my desire to play ball was stronger than ever and that baseball had become my way of life. She reluctantly agreed I should go.

Now here's what the White Sox told me: I would go up against another catcher named Sam Hairston during spring training. I knew Sam from 1948 when we were teammates in Indianapolis, along with Jackie. The better man would go to Colorado Springs, Colorado, and join Chicago's Class A farm team, the Rockies. The loser would go to Waterloo, Iowa, a Class C team.

Counting me and Hairston, six blacks were trying to make the team. They included Gideon Applegate and Gene Collins, a pitcher for the Kansas City Monarchs.

There was also Connie Johnson, another Monarch pitcher.

While we were together in Victoria, Texas, Connie gave me some extra details about a game in 1946, where I hit two home runs off of him in Philadelphia. My first time up, I smacked his first pitch into the left center field upper deck. My next at bat, I tomahawked one farther back than the first. I wasn't supposed to get a chance to hit that second one, he told me.

"You were supposed to go down," Connie said. Monarch manager Frank Duncan then threatened his pitcher. "He told me that if I didn't knock you down the next time you came up, I would be fined twenty-five dollars." Sure enough, I hit the dirt. We had a good laugh about that.

Being black and living in Texas was rough. We couldn't stay with the rest of the team. We had to live in the house of a black school teacher and her family, who gladly opened their doors to us. It was 1952, but we were in Texas, and change there came slowly. Very slowly.

Victoria was racist, but it was filthy rich. Some families had oil derricks pumping in their back yards earning royalties of twenty-five thousand dollars a month, I was told.

Don Gutridge was the manager in Victoria. He was a tough son of a gun. If you lost a game and came into the clubhouse whistling, he'd be on your case. "Who the hell has the nerve to be whistling!" he'd roar. "You should've put that energy out there on the damn field!"

He and Glenn Miller, secretary of the White Sox farm system, said my performance would determine whether I got to Colorado Springs. I thought these guys were serious. They had already shipped the mediocre players to another complex. They weren't going to waste time looking at those guys.

There would be twenty-nine exhibition games. At first they wanted Sam and me to split catching duties each game—he would catch four innings, I'd catch five. That was crazy. A good catcher develops a feel for the game he's in. To yank him in the middle of a game didn't make sense. "Let each catcher catch his own game," I said.

I had a good spring. I hit the ball hard, my arm was strong, and most importantly, the pitchers wanted me as their catcher. One day we went into Wichita Falls, Texas, and it was windy as heck. The flag in center field was blowing straight toward home plate. During one of my at-bats, I smacked a ball through that wind. The ball hit high off the fence, just two feet shy from going out of the park. Dumb old me, instead of legging out the hit, I admired it like Barry Bonds would and nearly got thrown out at second base. But that hit got people talking about my power. Hitting the ball that far against that strong wind—man, that impressed them.

We practiced one Tuesday, and the field was hard as cement. Our spikes barely cracked the infield dirt. When we looked up at Pikes Peak, we could see nothing but snow.

After practice, I felt this throbbing pain in my left leg. I limped to the clinic a half a block away, where the doctor met me at the door, grabbed my hand, and pumped it vigorously. "Bill, so glad to have ya," he said. "You've had a heck of a spring so far."

The praise was nice, but my leg was killing me. The doc took a look at it, and the news wasn't good. He said I had phlebitis, an inflammation of the veins. He wanted to put me in the hospital. He was crazy. I was fighting for a job.

"Doc, are you kidding? It's opening day tomorrow."

"You go into the hospital today, or I take that leg off next week."

My back was against the wall. The pain was tremendous, but one day away from the team meant one fewer opportunity to seal my chance of playing for Colorado Springs. I couldn't play with this leg. I couldn't even run.

I stayed in the hospital four days, with hot water bottles wrapped around my leg. When the bottles got cold, a nurse brought more in right away. I was itching to get back. So when the doctor came in Friday morning, I gave him a line about how Sam had too much to do, and that I could help warm up the pitchers. The doctor didn't want me to check out until Tuesday, but he agreed to discharge me Friday after I promised not to play ball. I wanted to be with the team when it went to Pueblo.

I kept my promise. I stayed in the bullpen, and we lost 5-2. We played them again the next day, and I was still in the bullpen. We were behind 5-0 in the seventh inning when Sam Hairston led off with a double off the left center field wall. Gutridge, who was coaching third base, called time and pointed to our bullpen in right field. I thought he was trying to get the attention of the pitchers. But he wanted me. I was to pitch run for Hairston.

Of all the times to be asked to pitch run. I hadn't run since Tuesday and was more than a little sore and stiff. So I did a couple of quick knee bends, which was also a signal that I would be watching the third base coach, and that was the extent of my warm-up. I jogged out to second base.

The next batter hit one up the middle. I took off for third, touched the bag, and rounded for home. I knew the throw from the outfield was going to be close, so I went into a fade-away slide. My sore leg crashed into the catcher's shin guard; bolts of pain shot up my leg. "Safe!" yelled the ump.

I stayed in the game. Pueblo scored twice in the seventh and once more in the eighth. It was turning into a blow out, but I got some revenge. In our half of the ninth, Willie Wells tripled. Then I came up and smashed little Marvin Williams' curveball into the crisp Colorado air. They're still looking for that ball.

After I showered and put my equipment away, I saw Gideon Applegate sitting on the bench, his head down. Everyone else had left the clubhouse. I wondered what was wrong. Then Gutridge came up to me. He kept looking at the floor.

"Bill, they want you to go to Waterloo," he said. Waterloo? The Class C team? I was confused. Wasn't the best player supposed to stay? Sam caught fifteen games and batted. .214. I caught fourteen, batted .375. The pitchers liked me. No catcher had an arm like mine. Shoot, in Terra Haute, I threw out a kid who had stolen fifty-four straight bases.

I said to him, "Wait a minute. You and Glenn Miller promised that the guy who came out on top would stay here."

"We know you showed up best," Gutridge said. "It's coming from the front office."

"Coming from the front office? I'm getting screwed, and you know it."

Gutridge and Glenn Miller, secretary of the White Sox farm system, had lied. Just outright lied. And Frank Lane, the White Sox general manager, had given them his blessing. I learned they had agreed to send Sam to Colorado Springs, no matter what happened in spring training. Sam had been with the White Sox briefly in 1951, becoming the first black to play for that organization. But just before the season was over, both catchers at Colorado Springs got hurt, so they sent Sam down.

You know why Gutridge and Miller brought me to Victoria? They wanted a good catcher for their lesser talented Waterloo team. They baited me. They knew I wouldn't come to play on some little league Class C team, not after I was the all-star catcher in the Provincial League.

That White Sox trick demoralized me. If you cross me once, I never forget it. Never. Now, I'm a Christian man, and I know you should forgive those who hurt you, but to this day, I hold bad feelings toward the White Sox. That's not healthy or righteous, but that's me.

Sam and I remained friends. Shoot, he had nothing to do with that mess in Victoria, Texas. Right after Gutridge gave me the bad news that day, I left the locker room and went out to the team bus and sought out Sam. I shook his hand.

"Don't look back," I said to him. "I'm going to be on your butt like white on rice."

Later, Gideon and I were on a train to Waterloo.

The Waterloo team was coached by Skeeter Webb, a no-nonsense baseball man who didn't take no stuff from nobody.

"Whatever Cash calls for, you throw it," he told the young pitchers, most of them just out of high school. They paid attention for the most part, but there was this one guy who knew everything.

His name was Terry Loy. He was six feet four inches, 210 pounds, and could throw a ball through a brick wall. Trouble was, he didn't know what part of the wall the ball was going to hit. I worked with him and tried to slow him down until he learned control. But he was hardheaded.

One game, he took a 6-0 lead into the third inning then tried to blow the ball by everybody. Soon it was 7-6. And that seventh run came after I called for a curveball and Terry threw a fastball. Skeeter had seen enough. He met us at the third base foul line.

"What happened?"

"I figured I could get my fastball right by him," Terry said.

"So why the hell didn't you throw it?!"

Or Terry could've shaken me off. You know, I never understood pitchers who ignored a catcher's signs. If you don't like the pitch, just shake it off until he signals you a pitch you do like. Otherwise I'm expecting the ball to go one way—and bam—it goes another. That's how my fingers got so messed up, trying to adjust at the last minute and keep the ball from getting away from me.

So Terry, the promising flame-thrower, who was given a forty thousand-dollar contract, got sent out after that game. He never made the pros.

I took pride in staying in shape, but in 1952 my body rebelled. After suffering the phlebitis in my leg, I got bursitis in my shoulder while in Waterloo. The pain was so bad I had to support my arm when I shaved. Swinging the bat was tough. To top it off, I pulled a muscle in my leg.

My batting average nosedived from .340 to .240. The bursitis bothered me for about a week. Then the pulled muscle kept me out three more weeks.

While I was injured, they brought in some kid right fielder to catch. I didn't know it at the time, but they paid him a forty thousand-dollar bonus. His big chance came against a team from Cedar Rapids, Iowa, that had Art Pennington. I knew Art. I had played with him in Mexico and knew how to get him out. But they wouldn't listen to me. Art got eleven hits in the three-game series and won the league batting title.

Then there was that three-city swing through the southern Midwest: Evansville, Indiana, Terra Haute, Indiana, and Quincy, Illinois. Talk about lowdown racism. While my white teammates stayed in nice hotels in those cities, my black teammates and I stayed in the homes of black preachers.

Now don't get me wrong. The preachers were wonderful and took us in with open arms. And I had stayed in private homes before. But here I am—the best ballplayer on the team and they relegate you like that. It was demoralizing. I was just outdone. And Skeeter didn't say a word.

We handled it the way we always did. We went out and played ball.

By June 13, 1952—shoot, I'll never forget that date— Skeeter got some backbone. We were in Davenport, Iowa, of all places. The stadium there sat so close to the Mississippi River that if you hit a ball hard to right field, it could splash into the river's locks. They threw sawdust in the outfield to soak up the water that spilled over from the locks that controlled the mighty river.

Anyway, Skeeter told the hotel manager in Davenport, "I want all my ballplayers to be together." And so we black players were finally able to stay in the same hotel as the white players. I don't know what made Davenport so different from Evansville, Terra Haute, or Quincy. Skeeter got some courage when it came to off-the-field issues, but I'll never understand why he didn't go to bat for us sooner.

One Friday night in Evansville symbolized my stay. I came up with the bases loaded in the seventh inning and got a single. Next batter up, Skeeter called for a hit-and-run. I was off with the pitch. When I slid into second base, I felt a sharp pain in my leg. I looked down and saw my foot twisted at an ugly right angle. My leg was broke.

The team doctor rushed out of the dugout. I tried to stand, but he shoved me back down to the infield dirt. He set my leg right there on second base. Twenty-five minutes later, I was in the hospital, my leg in a cast.

Saturday morning, the doctor came into my room and gave the OK to go home. So I got on my crutches, hobbled to the airport, and flew home, tired and aching. Sadie was in New York visiting Hank Thompson and his wife, so when I landed in Philadelphia, I disguised my voice, called my mother's house, and asked for my brother Art. I needed someone to pick me up, and I didn't want my mother to know I was in town. She was upset enough that I had hurt myself. Art came down and took me home.

I was out nine weeks. And you know something? I didn't even have to slide on that play. I later found out that when the ball was hit to first baseman Horace Gardner, he didn't bother to throw it to second. That sneaky little shortstop Felix Mantilla, who later played for the Red Sox, pretended he was catching the ball, so I slid to avoid a tag that never came.

Later I heard they had planned to send me to Colorado Springs after that Southern swing. They were selling Sam Hairston to Portland in the Pacific Coast League, and I would've moved up. But my broken leg blew the deal.

On my trip back to Waterloo two months later, I brought Sadie, Billy, and Janet. We stopped in Chicago to visit a cousin. There was some parade in town that Sadie and the kids just *had* to see. I told them OK, but don't be too long, because we still had to travel three hundred miles to Waterloo and I wanted to be there before nightfall.

Well, they came back from the parade around three in the afternoon. I was so hot you could've fried a dozen eggs on me. We hurriedly packed the car and took off, getting to Waterloo about 11 p.m. I didn't have any reservations and no hotel rooms were available at that hour. So we stayed with a friend, Vi Norman, his wife and family. I had stayed with Vi's family the first time I was in Waterloo. They were so kind, even at that hour. Vi and his wife fixed beds for the kids and then let me and Sadie sleep in their own bed.

We stayed a week, because the team was away on a Southern swing. I arrived in Waterloo on August 5, but I later found out I was supposed to be in town August 1. No one had bothered to tell me.

Since the team was away, I helped out Vi in his supermarket like I did the year before. One day while

I was outside exercising, the team's secretary came out and told me I had a phone call. It was Skeeter Webb.

"Bill, they need you in Superior, Wisconsin," Skeeter said. The Superior Blues was another Chicago White Sox farm team in the Northern League. "They're leading the league by twelve games, but Eau Claire and Sioux Falls are breathing down their necks. Plus both catchers are hurt." Skeeter said that because I reported late, I would be ineligible for the playoffs with Waterloo anyway.

"I'm not going," I said, surprising Skeeter. "They lied to me."

After everything I had been through with this organization, I wasn't eager to bail out their butts. I was tired of these games. Skeeter was in a tight spot. He handed the phone to Glenn Miller.

"I'm not going," I told him. "You all lied to me about Colorado Springs. You all could've told me the truth. I would've worked just as hard."

"If you don't go," Glenn said in a stern voice, "I'm going to blackball you."

So it had come to this. If I didn't dance to their tune, they'd find a way to stop the music. With that darn reserve clause, they could do just that. I wasn't a Negro Leaguer anymore. I was no longer a free agent who could bounce from team to team whenever the money or opportunity was right. The Chicago White Sox had their claws in my chest and could fling me anywhere they wanted. If I flat-out refused, my chance of making the majors was doomed. But I had also signed a contract to play winter ball in Mexico. So if this Superior thing didn't work out, I was still covered.

"When do you want me there?"

I got into Superior two days later, with a brace on my leg. I pulled up to the ballpark about 4 p.m. Saturday. The grounds keeper directed me to the Y, where they had an apartment ready for me and my family.

The team arrived at the ballpark around 6 p.m. During that night's game, Sadie was sitting in the stands when this white woman came over to her. "We have seats over here," she told Sadie. The white woman was the wife of a teammate.

So she and Sadie got to talking. "Are there any black people in this town?" Sadie asked.

"I'm the only one," said the woman. Well, Sadie just about fell out of her chair. Her new friend was biracial. Her mother was white; her father was black.

The season was nearly at an end when I took over catching from a young white guy named Brofy. He was such a lousy batter he couldn't hit me if I walked across the plate. The manager pitch hit for him during a game with Eau Claire, a team from Wisconsin that was a farm club for the Milwaukee Braves. The pitch hitter, Gideon Applegate, singled, and I was Brofy's defensive replacement. Brofy never caught another game with the Blues.

In the tournament to reach the Northern League championship round, we played Eau Claire. We had won two games at home and made the trip to their place. Playing for Eau Claire was an eighteen-year-old phenom outfielder who was hitting .336 and had the pro scouts excited.

His name was Henry Aaron.

We're leading 4-3 going into the bottom of the ninth. They had a man on second, and up to bat was Hank. He fouled off five or six pitches with that powerful swing of his. He was tough, but I saw something in his young eyes and in his swing. I called time out and walked to the pitching mound to talk to our hurler, who was Cuban.

"Throw him that slider," I said in Spanish, "and make sure it starts at his ribs." The next pitch came right at Hank's ribs. He backed off the plate and stared as the ball broke across the plate for the third strike.

We won the game and the tournament. But as you all know, Hank went on to much bigger and better things. He was named the Northern League's Rookie of the Year in 1952 and made it to its all-star team.

You know Hank hit 755 home runs for the Braves in Milwaukee and Atlanta, and for the Milwaukee Brewers, becoming the greatest home-run hitter in major league baseball history. When he sent Al Downing's fastball out of Atlanta Stadium on April 8, 1974, he ended any arguments about the skill and quality of black baseball players. Hank that night overtook the biggest, whitest icon in baseball history, Babe Ruth. Jackie Robinson put the nail in the mythical coffin in 1947. Hank hammered it home in 1974.

Nineteen fifty-two, a year that started with thoughts of me playing major league baseball, ended on an anti-climatic note. The Blues handled the Sioux Falls threat by winning. When we traveled to play them in the championship series, we were so confident we left our toothbrushes home.

For those eighteen- and nineteen-year-old kids, winning the Northern League Championship was a big deal. They were thrilled. They had never won anything like this before, so they really celebrated. On the trip back to Superior, one kid was so drunk he threw up all over the bus.

The win didn't mean much to me. I had played with some of baseball's best. I had traveled to exotic locales and had done things these kids could only dream of. Winning the Northern League title for a low-level mid-Western farm team didn't mean nothing to me. The kids drank beer and whooped it up. I drank an orange soda and fell asleep.

The next night, the White Sox organization had a banquet at a Superior restaurant in honor of the team. Sadie, Billy, and Janet were there—gosh, I missed them so much—and had a good time. But we had to get back to Philadelphia quickly. Billy and Janet had to be back in school in two days. And we didn't want to miss that.

At ten the next morning, we piled into my 1950 Pontiac and hit the road. We had to cover one thousand one hundred miles in two days. Sadie had arranged the back seat so Billy and Janet could sleep there.

Man, I loved the Pontiac. It was my first-ever new car and had one of those straight-8 engines that moved! My foot stayed planted on the accelerator. By seven the next morning, we were in Chicago. We went to get something to eat, but I was tired. I told Sadie she should drive for a while.

Sadie had just gotten her driver's license. I told her to stay on Route 30, and that would take us straight to the Pennsylvania Turnpike. Everything seemed OK, so I fell asleep.

Minutes later, I was awakened by the roar of the car engine switching into high gear. I couldn't believe my eyes. Sadie had gotten behind an eighteen-wheeler and was trying to pass it on a two-lane highway. And there was another eighteen-wheeler barreling down the oncoming lane! She swung the car back into her lane, keeping us from getting smashed to smithereens.

Shoot, I took over the driving duties after that. Back then, my wife was a better cosmetologist than driver. We stopped a couple of times at rest areas in Indiana. Sadie would lay out a blanket, and I'd fall right to sleep while Billy and Janet played around me.

When I was on the road, I was doing eighty-five to ninety miles per hour. The troopers didn't bother you like they do now. Every once in a while, I pulled over to the side of the road, got out, and did some exercises. Sadie, Billy, and Janet thought I was crazy, but I thought it was important to stretch and keep the blood flowing after driving so long. Plus it helped me stay awake.

Around midnight on the Pennsylvania Turnpike, I pulled into a service station to get the Pontiac lubed and its oil changed. That was an odd time for vehicle maintenance, but I truly believe if you take good care of a car, it'll take good care of you. Back in those days I got an oil job and lube for my car every one thousand two hundred miles. So far on this trip, my Pontiac was taking care of us just fine, thank you. We were still several hours away from home, and I wanted to be sure we got there without a problem.

I didn't want to waste time either. So when the guys put the car on the lift, me, Sadie, and the kids stayed inside and slept. The nap helped. We got to Philadelphia 8 a.m. on Friday. The kids were two days late for school, but that was OK. Sadie took them to school because I could barely walk. I tumbled into bed and slept, mission accomplished.

CHAPTER 10

STAYING ON THE DIAMOND

✳ ✳ ✳

You can only milk a cow so long, then you're left holding the pail.
— Henry Aaron, Hall of Fame outfielder

I still had my job at the Lester Piano Company in 1953, but it wasn't the end-all, be-all of my existence. Baseball was in my blood. I had played semi-pro and pro for thirteen years. I wanted to prove something.

But organized baseball's reserve clause kept me handcuffed to the White Sox organization. You could play in the Latin countries because they weren't part of the major league system at the time, but I couldn't make a move in organized baseball without the White Sox's OK. They could do anything they wanted to—send you down to the minors and keep you from jumping to another team. I mean, it was like slavery all over again. And all of this with an organization I detested.

I had to get out from under this reserve-clause thing.

In '53, I went back north to play with the Brandon, Manitoba Braves in Canada's Man-Dak League. Canada still had that specialness I loved. They judged you by your character, not your skin color.

Man-Dak is shorthand for the province of Manitoba and the state of North Dakota. The league was small,

140 THOU SHALT NOT STEAL

but a good place to find prospects. It included teams from Winnipeg, Brandon, another Canadian city whose name skips my mind, and Minnot, North Dakota. My teammates included a couple of guys who played for the Phillies, Bill Hockleberry and Ken Sylvester.

After three months, I led the Man-Dak league in hitting, with a .392 average. Then I got a call from a team in the Dominican Republic.

In the 1930s, '40s, and '50s, the Dominican Republic was an outlaw league. Uncle Sam had a tough time dealing with that country. Politics literally came on the baseball field when Rafael Trujillo, dictator of the Dominican Republic, sponsored his own team called Ciudad Trujillo. Man, this guy had an ego. And to help himself win, he snatched the best players from the Negro Leagues. Truth be told, if we had to choose between politics and a paycheck, money won hands down.

Satchel seldom saw a dollar sign he didn't like. He jumped the Pittsburgh Crawfords to go to the Dominican Republic in the summer of 1937. Later a few of his friends joined him: Josh, Sam Bankhead, and some other Crawford guys. It didn't take long for the Negro League grapevine to start crackling about the big bucks Satch and those guys were getting.

But I'm glad I didn't get there till a few years later. Satch said armed guards threatened him and other teammates, saying they'd better win or something bad would happen to them. Then there's a story that Trujillo once put his ballplayers in jail so they couldn't do any carousing before a big game. That year so much money was paid to the Trujillo players that pro ball in the Dominican Republic suffered and didn't resurface in an organized way until 1951.

In 1953, I was with the Braves in Manitoba when a team in the Dominican Republic called and wanted to know how much money it would take to lure me there. I said two thousand five hundred dollars a month, plus expenses.

With a month up front, of course.

They just about had a fit. I can imagine what they were thinking. *Twenty-five hundred a month? Plus expenses? Who does this guy think he is, the second coming of Josh Gibson?* The guy I was dealing with didn't think I was worth the money.

A week later I went down to the Dominican Republic to play for the Aegis Bandits for one thousand five hundred dollars a month, plus expenses. I took a pay cut, but the money was still good, and I would be playing in a competitive league.

But before the season started, the Bandits directors wanted to meet at one of the country's plush tennis clubs. When I arrived, I was greeted by some little lawyer who took me into a back room, where the other directors were gathered. The Bandits needed an outfielder, they said, and wanted me to do some recruiting. "We want you to get Art Pennington."

I wanted Art too, but I had to have a backup plan in case I couldn't pull him away from the Cedar Rapids team. If Art couldn't make it, I'd go to Canada and get Joe Atkins, who had played with the Pittsburgh Crawfords and Cleveland Buckeyes.

But I knew Art was available. The Bandits gave me an expense account, two round-trip airplane tickets, a nine hundred-dollar check made out to Art that could only be cashed in the Dominican Republic, and two hundred dollars cash for Art's wife, Anita. That money would tie her over until Art cashed the check and could send more money back to her in the States.

Early the next morning, a cab picked me up and took me to the Ciudad Trujillo Airport. My first flight was overbooked, so after some delay, I finally arrived at Idlewild Airport in New York and met the team's state-side contact, a white man, who drove me back to his house. The contact man was in a hurry to get to his other job and couldn't stay. So he let me use his phone to call Art's mother in Hot Springs, Arkansas. She could get me in touch with Art.

The contact man left me alone with his wife. Let me tell you, in those days that was a rare thing for a white man to do, almost unheard of, leave his wife alone with a Negro man. But I guess he trusted me. And I haven't forgotten that.

Art had written me earlier, saying he had borrowed five hundred dollars from the Cedar Rapids team. The team wanted its money back and knew Art was hot to play in Latin countries. But the team owners had so much power that if anyone tried to contact Art, they would put them in jail.

I called Art's mother three or four times in Hot Springs, but no luck. I checked into the Woodside Hotel, one of the most famous hotels in Harlem. Many visiting Negro League teams stayed there over the years—it was about the only place they were allowed.

I had a 3 p.m. flight out of La Guardia, so I told the operator to keep ringing that number every half-hour, and if she got through, to reach me at the bank. It was around 2 p.m. I figured I'd go there, cash Art's check, and give the money to Joe Atkins, because it didn't look like Art and I were going to connect.

The cashier said I couldn't cash the check. But while I was at the bank, I got a phone call. "Anyone here know Bill Cash?" hollered a bank employee.

Sure enough, it was Art.

"Look, I have a nine hundred-dollar check for you, plus two hundred dollars for Anita."

"That sounds good to me," Art said. "I'm going to tell the boys I'm leaving the team."

"Don't tell nobody," I nearly shouted at him. "You know what the owners told you. I don't want to go to jail. Look, when you come home from your game tonight, I'll be sitting in your parlor."

I rushed out the door and hailed the first cab I saw. "Woodside Hotel, 141st and Seventh Avenue," I said. It was the cabbie's first day on the job. He had no idea where the Woodside was.

I jumped out and bolted down the subway steps. I got off at 135th Street and Lenox Avenue, rushed up the steps, and spotted another cabbie. "Woodside, 141st and Seventh Avenue!"

The cabbie was startled. "Man, my transmission is acting up," he said. So I was thinking, *Ain't this a crying shame? It's just after 2 p.m. My flight leaves at three.*

I finally made it back to the hotel, packed my bags, paid my bill, and dashed out the door, It's 2:25. I flagged down a cab. "If you can make it to La Guardia in thirty minutes, you've got a big tip coming," I told him. Well, the cabbie put the pedal to the metal, but just as we arrived at the airport, I saw the United Airlines plane take off.

This recruiting stuff was driving me nuts.

I rushed to the airline counter. They had a 3:30 flight that stopped over in Chicago. I took it and pulled up to

Art's house in Cedar Rapids around 9:00 that night. Art was still at the ballpark, but his beautiful wife, Anita, a Mexican woman whose hair was so long she could sit on it, made me feel welcome. Art finally got home, and we went to a restaurant where nobody could recognize us—he didn't want anyone to know he was jumping the team. We ate and talked, and then I checked into a hotel.

We left at eight the next morning for New York. I put Art in the Woodside while I went to Philadelphia to see Sadie and the kids.

Now Art used to take his nickname "Superman" to heart when it came to the women, especially white women. So when I knocked on his door at the Woodside, ready to take him to the airport, I found him laid up with a little cutie. "Man, we ain't got time for that now," I said.

When we landed at the Cuidad Trujillo Airport, all of the Bandits directors were waiting anxiously at the gate. The airplane hatch opened, and Art and I just stood there, shoulder to shoulder. The directors let up a cheer.

Art was with the team only one-and-a-half months, but he helped us finish in second place. I hit .367 in the Dominican Republic league. One day I was feeling my oats. I just had a great season, and I was giving the Bandits a good bang for their bucks.

"Was I worth it?" I asked manager Rudolph Fernandez.

"Hell, yeah, you were worth it."

I played out the season, came home, and then went back to the Mexican Pacific Coast League to play for

Obregon. That's when the strangest thing happened. In the first game of a day-night series against Los Mochis, a foul tip broke the finger next to my pinkie finger on my right hand. That happened in the fifth inning, but I finished the game. I came back that night and caught the entire second game.

The next day I went to the local hospital, but I might as well have stayed home. Instead of putting my finger in a splint, they wrapped it in a Band-Aid. Can you believe that? My finger healed but was never the same. It's tilted at an odd angle. I missed only one game, but my batting average dropped from .343 to .258. I couldn't catch with a broken finger, so I played right field, where at least my arm could still do some good.

Meanwhile Obregon owner Javier Bours hired Clint Courtney of the St. Louis Browns to be catcher and manager, paying him twice the money I was getting. Then Bours got the great Don Larsen of the New York Yankees. In the 1956 World Series against the Brooklyn Dodgers, Larsen would become the first person in series history to pitch a perfect game. We already had Al Heiss and Buddy Peterson on our roster, bringing the number of foreigners on Obregon to five, the maximum allowed on Mexican Pacific Coast League teams.

The day after I broke my finger, Bours looked at my X-rays and started making noises. My average kept dropping, and newspaper stories started appearing, saying he was going to release me. Just like that. It didn't matter that I had been the league's all-star catcher for four years. Nobody in the front office had the guts to say one word to me. I learned about the trade stories from a teammate on a Monday. I stormed into Bours' office that day and asked for my release. He told me to hold off on any decision until Clint and the other fellows returned from a fishing trip.

When Clint got back, he tried to convince me to stay. He said I'd be right back catching once my finger healed. But I told him I had read the newspapers, and I didn't want to play for a team that didn't want me.

Once the word was out that Obregon wanted to get rid of me, four other teams—Hermosillo, Navojoa, Los Mochis, and Guaymas—called offering me a spot on their rosters. I tallied the pluses and minuses of each team and city. Navojoa was still pretty rural. If it rained there, you were stuck in the mud. Los Mochis no longer had its star player, Marvin Williams. Now Guaymas did have a great restaurant, Mammy's, which sold the biggest and tastiest shrimp you ever ate. But I settled on Hermosillo. It was the most modern of the four cities with paved streets and a canal that served the rancheros.

The rest of that week, my finger grew stronger. Saturday night and Sunday morning, I still struggled at the plate. But on Sunday night, everything came together. I hit a single, a double, and a home run. The next day I went into Bours' office and got my release. I wasted no time returning to my hotel and calling Hermosillo.

"We'll send a cab down for you, Bill," they said. When I reached the ballpark, the Hermosillo ballplayers greeted me with open arms. That sure felt good.

Hermosillo was having problems with this one young Mexican player. I can't remember his name. He had a lot of power but was only hitting .258. The manager was at his wit's end. He didn't know what to do with the guy.

I took the kid under my wing, worked with him during practice, helped him with his stance, but mostly gave him encouragement. I told the coach to let him hit behind me.

I clearly recall one game Hermosillo played that year against Obregon, which had added Frank Sullivan of the Boston Red Sox to its roster since I left. We were heavy underdogs to lose all four games in the series. Things sure started out that way.

On Friday night, Sullivan beat us 9-2. On Saturday night, Don Larsen was pitching. In my first time up, I swung way out in front of a Larsen change up. A swing and a miss like that can be mighty embarrassing. Clint Courtney, who was catching, laughed so hard he fell on the ground. Larsen thought he had my number, but neither he nor Clint saw what I did next: I widened my stance. Larsen tried the same pitch again, and I stroked a solid single.

By the eighth inning, Larsen was beating us 6-0. We got three runs and went into the ninth trailing 6-3. During our at-bat, our shortstop, little David, got a single.

Then Chunky Londias, our center fielder, came up and hit the ball a ton. Man, we all thought it was leaving the park, but Al Heiss flagged it down in left center for a long out. Then Larsen got cocky. He was so sure he had the game won, he didn't go into a stretch to hold little David on. He just started pumping and little David started running—to second base. Ball one to our third baseman, Nigro Rodriquez.

Larsen looked at second base and pumped again. Little David took off again, stealing third. Ball two. On the next pitch Rodriquez banged a high chopper over

Larsen's head that neither the second baseman nor shortstop could handle. Little David trotted home. So now we're at 6-4.

That brought me up to the plate. I had figured Larsen out. I settled in and cracked a homer over the right center field scoreboard, tying the game at 6. The fans went crazy.

Then it was that troubled young player's turn. As he walked to the batter's box, I told him, "*No espersa nada*"—"Don't wait for nothing." He dug in, swung, and sent Larsen's first pitch over the fence. We won 7-6. And you know what? After three months, his batting average had reached .361.

I impressed Clint during that series. In a game the day after we beat Don Larsen, I was catching and Al Heiss was on first. I called for a curveball and the Mexican pitcher threw it in the dirt. Well, Heiss was off and running. I "nut hopped" the pitch, dug it out the dirt, and fired the ball to second base, a foot off the ground. Heiss was out. I never left my crouch.

Clint stopped the game, walked over to me, and shook my hand. "Bill, that's the greatest throw I have ever seen in my life," he said. "If I could catch, hit, and throw like you, I'd be the greatest thing the America League ever had."

"I'm the property of the Chicago White Sox," I told Clint. "They won't bring me up because I'm black."

Like many other cities in Mexico, Hermosillo was full of ducks. Sometimes there were so many birds they blocked out the sun. The team owner's son drove a convertible and liked to hunt. So every now and then, I'd take the wheel and drive along the canal while he leaned out of the car and fired away at the ducks. Then we'd take them home and have us a good meal. Man, those ducks could weigh up to four pounds apiece.

One day my friends Barney Brown and Howard Easterling, who were playing for Navojoa, came up to Obregon to visit me. They went out, set the shotgun's butt on the ground, pointed the barrel in the air, and fired twice. Forty-two ducks fell tumbling out of the sky. Forty-two! And let me tell you, Barney could cook up some duck. You just had to be careful not to bite into a shotgun pellet.

Animals in Mexico could put a hurting on your car. Cows, horses, deer, and jack rabbits that stood waist high often wandered onto the roads—especially Highway 15 from Nogales to Mexico City—and wound up denting your fender, shattering your car windshield. Or becoming road kill.

At the end of the Pacific Coast League season in March 1954, Art Pennington and I decided to come home for a few months before returning to the Dominican Republic. They finally got organized baseball down there. No more of that outlaw league talk.

But that trip Art and I took from Mexico back to the States was something else. Art and I always seemed to wind up taking some strange journey. This time we agreed to meet up in Nogales and drive to Hot Springs, Arkansas. But even before we got out of Mexico, the car's alternator went bad, and we had to get a tow truck to take us to a garage.

Then it started pouring rain. We decided to keep the car in the garage until the storm blew over. We finally left Nogales around 12:30 p.m., and that night we were going through the mountains. Man, that was a long trip.

The speedometer might have said we were traveling fifty miles per hour, but it felt like thirty, those hills were so steep. There were signs posted along the road warning travelers not leave their cars because of mountain lions. Yeah, that was real reassuring.

I was really eager to get home because I wanted to see my youngest son, Michael, who was born while I was away playing ball. Once we got to Hot Springs, Art wanted me to stay with him. No way, I said, I had a new son I hadn't seen. I caught a train from Hot Springs to Philly and finally got to see Michael.

When I went back to the Dominican Republic later that year, I went to play for another team, Licey. But I should've just stayed home.

Talk about out of shape. Now, you know I took pride in my exercise routine and in staying fit, but I had enjoyed my time home a bit too much. Eating, laying around, playing with the kids. And it showed. Guys I had smacked homers off a few months ago were striking me out. And the Licey owners weren't patient. They shipped me home after about a month.

In the spring of '54, I was asked to be a player/manager down in the Dominican Republic for the Santiago Eagles. Alex, the team's general manager, stayed on me about the job. For some reason, they weren't happy with their current manager, Rudolfo Fernandez, who had been the Bandits manager when I played with them. I had no problem with Rudolfo. He was a decent man, didn't yell or scream at his players. And he was very knowledgeable about the game. But for some reason, they didn't want him.

I kept telling Alex I wasn't interested, that it was too hard trying to catch and manage. He said they'd increase my pay. But I wasn't worried about the money. I just didn't want to do all that thinking a good catcher does plus worry about the players on the field.

I guess they were desperate. They offered me an additional four hundred dollars, jacking the salary to one thousand nine hundred dollars a month—plus expenses. And when I heard that Luis Olmo of the Dodgers would be my left fielder, I gave in. But I wanted certain conditions. Many of the team's twenty-two directors were lawyers with reputations for getting too involved with on-field decisions. I wanted to nip that stuff in the bud.

"When that ball team is on the field, it's my team," I told them. "I don't want to see any of you out there."

They agreed. And I signed the contract.

Before the season started, Alex said we needed some more players, especially pitchers. So I was back to recruiting. I went to Miami and stayed at the Lord Culvert Hotel, the black hotel on Third Street, which we used as a base of operations. We were looking everywhere for other talent too, so Alex flew to Cuba to try to get Orestes "Minnie" Minoso to play third for us. He didn't have any luck.

When Alex returned to Miami, I told him I needed a car. Sadie and Michael had come down, and we planned to visit Sadie's mother, Mom Clark, over in South Miami. I was on an expense sheet, so paying for a car was no problem. But trying to rent one was.

Alex didn't have a driver's license that could be used in the United States, so he couldn't rent a car. "Come on, let's go around the corner to the Hertz office," I told him. "I have an American driver's license. They can rent one to me."

We arrived at the office and this cracker treated me like I was some kid. "Who's going to be responsible for the car?" he asked in a whiny, high-pitched voice.

"Me," I answered.

He looked at me and shook his head "no." He couldn't have made it more plain: I was a black man in white America. I knew nothing about responsibility. Alex and I stormed out.

The Lord Culvert Hotel's manager, Mr. Ferguson, heard about my experience. He got on the phone and called Avis, Hertz's competition. The difference was like night and day. In fifteen minutes I had a brand new 1954 Chevy to drive. Since that day, all of my car rentals have been through Avis. I'm a loyal customer because they treated me as Bill Cash the person, not Bill Cash the black man.

Back in the Dominican Republic, man, those Eagles owners wouldn't leave me alone. I had a hint that things weren't going to be good when I picked the starting lineup. There was this kid named Ted Tenao, who played winter ball in Puerto Rico. I guess he thought that because he played in Puerto Rico, he should be the team's starting center fielder. But I had another little kid named Martinez, who ran like a farm bird, so he was nicknamed "Gallo," which is Spanish for rooster. He could field and hit, but he didn't have Tenao's baseball fundamentals.

I had watched these guys for two weeks during training. When opening day came, Gallo beat out Tenao for the center field spot. Tenao was mad and went around bad-mouthing me, telling anyone who would listen that I was a lousy manager. And word was getting to the directors. I had a good friend in the Dominican

Republic whom I considered my "godfather." He was an importer—just about everything that came into the country had to go through his business—and one of the richest men in the Western Hemisphere. He had connections to the team. And he wanted to know why Gallo was starting over Tenao.

"Gallo's a better ballplayer," I said. My godfather let it go at that.

We lost the opening game on Saturday afternoon and the next game on Sunday morning. I was making out the lineup for our Sunday afternoon game when one of the directors, a short, smart-aleck lawyer with money to burn, came out on the field and asked me who was pitching.

"None of your business! When the announcer announces the pitcher, then you'll know!"

Shoot, I didn't need this nonsense. Everybody thought they were a darn manager. It was hard enough keeping track of batters and making defensive moves. That's why I didn't want anybody in my hair while I managed. I had reached the boiling point. "After this game," I told him, "get yourself another manager."

Well, this caused a stir in the little old Dominican Republic. News of my quitting was all over the television and radio. That Monday, my godfather called me and I went to his office to visit him. I told him the story. "Don't worry about it," he said. "If we get into the playoffs, you'll get your money. Now go to the warehouse and tell Jose you want two suits. And that I'm paying for 'em."

So I went there and ordered two English-worsted suits, the best around. And you know something? Three weeks later, the darn league folded. The league had had high hopes—it had even built a new stadium because it was planning to go into organized baseball—but it wasn't drawing enough people to the games.

I returned to the Dominican Republic for a short stint as a manager of San Diego; then in September, I went back to play again for Obregon in the Mexican Pacific Coast League.

Al "Sy" Cihocki's call in February 1955 surprised me. Sy, who played seven years with the Baltimore Orioles, saw me play while in the Dominican Republic. He got an offer to manage the Bismarck Barons in North Dakota and needed a catcher.

"If the money's right," I told Sy, "you got a man."

But the Barons' owner was only going to pay six hundred dollars a month, a big drop from what I was making in the Dominican Republic.

About a week later, I got a call from Mr. Wickland, owner of the Barons. "Sy told me what a heck of a catcher you are, but six hundred dollars is our limit. If we give you more than six hundred dollars, we'll have to let somebody else go."

"Mr. Wickland, I have nothing to do with that. Look, if you want me, you pay my price. I'm not like a lot of other guys. I'll stick to the terms of the contract. If I'm playing well, I won't come into your office and ask you to tear up my contract. But if I do good, I'm looking for a raise next year."

We settled on seven hundred fifty dollars a month and I had to be in Bismarck two weeks before the season started. The team had some youngsters who needed schooling.

Bismarck was a small farm town whose residents depended on wheat and barley crops for income. I remember driving along the highway out there and being fascinated by those big combines churning away in the fields.

Mr. Wickland took me around to community meetings—the Lions Club, Chamber of Commerce, stuff like that, so we could stir interest in the team.

I was never shy speaking in front of a crowd. Now I hadn't seen any of the players on this team, but for some reason, I felt we were going to be good. And that's what I told anybody who would listen. "We are going to be champs."

I didn't know the team was going to have Ray Dandridge and Jonas Gaines. Dandridge, one of the top third basemen to play in the Negro Leagues, was getting a little old, but still had the skills. Gaines had been a star left-handed pitcher for the Baltimore Elite Giants.

But we needed a center fielder, and I knew just the person. I gave my friend Art Pennington a call. Along with the call, I gave him a little advice. "You're too good a ballplayer to let these people soak you. I'm making seven hundred fifty dollars. You tell them whatever your price is, but don't let them get you for less than six hundred dollars."

Art came on board for six hundred dollars, and we were ready to roll. Art and I decided to move into a trailer. But later in the season, Art's wife and kids came to live in town, so I just let Art and his family stay in the trailer while I moved into another one.

We had four blacks on that team, and we were all doing well. Three weeks into the season, the Barons were 6-0 and I was leading the league, batting .392. We had a doctor and Rhodes Scholar, Mike Lotz, as a pitcher. When he wasn't pitching, his nose was stuck

inside a thick book. When the team was off, Lotz would
scrub and go into a local hospital operating room to
keep his surgical skills sharp. I think Detroit had even
offered him thirty-five thousand dollars to play in the
majors, but Lotz turned them down.

Everyone seemed to be having a good season. When
we reached 6-0, right fielder Ken Burkhart jumped and
went to St. Jobe, Minnesota, where he became manager
or something. He quickly made Lotz an offer to join
him. Lotz went into the Bismarck owners' office and
got a new contract for more money. When we hit 8-0,
Burkhart made Lotz another offer to play in Minnesota.
Lotz went into the owners' office and got another
contract.

Our left fielder, I think his name was Bill Jankowski,
was hitting .290 and *he* went and tore up his contract.
Everybody was playing well and getting compensated
for it. Everybody, it seemed, except me. But I had made
a promise—I would stick to my original contract.

But the dream season ended miserably. We won
the division but got knocked out of the playoffs in four
straight games.

I finished the seventy-game season with fifteen home
runs, sixty-nine RBIs, and a spot on the all-star team. My
.369 average set a record for catchers in the league. No
catcher since the famous Quincy Trouppe, who hit .319
back in the 1930s, has had as high an average in that
league.

So you can imagine my surprise when the next year
I got my contract from Bismarck in the mail and found
they wanted to pay me two hundred fifty dollars *less* per
month. I mean, you could've had a hundred bags of
confetti with all the player contracts they tore up the

previous season. A week later, Mr. Wickland called and wanted to know why I hadn't return the contract. Was he serious?

"Remember the conversation we had before I signed last year, Mr. Wickland? I told you I wouldn't come in and demand a new contract in the middle of the season, no matter how well I was playing. I would only ask for a raise after the season if I played well. I stuck to that. Now I set a record, I'm an all-star catcher in the league, and you want to cut my pay? I'm looking for a raise."

"We can't afford it, Bill," Wickland said.

Well, I guess not, I thought to myself. *You gave everybody a darn raise last year and now you want to make up the difference by cutting my pay.* So I said, "Well, I guess you don't need me. Thank you."

I hung up the phone, tore up the contract, and tossed it in the trash can.

This reserve clause had gone too far, and I needed to get free. It was obvious the White Sox didn't give a darn about me anymore and were willing to let me wither away. A friend of mine suggested I get the local Masonic grand master to write a letter asking for my release. I had been involved with the Masons since 1951, but I never thought about testing the limits of the brotherhood this way. But shoot, I had nothing to lose. The grand master was William Grasty. He sat down and wrote letters to the White Sox, to the Waterloo club, and a few other places seeking my release.

And don't you know, it worked.

Curt Flood of the St. Louis Cardinals had the guts to take the reserve clause to a higher level. When Curt was traded to the Philadelphia Phillies in 1969 after being with St. Louis for twelve seasons, he refused to go and challenged the clause in federal court. He said the clause was unconstitutional and violated anti-trust laws.

"After twelve years in the major leagues, I do not feel that I am a piece of property to be bought and sold irrespective of my wishes," Curt wrote to baseball commissioner Bowie Kuhn in December 1969. The first team to sign you could do whatever the heck it wanted to with you. And to top it off, you were bound to that team forever. "It was a master and slave relationship," Curt would later say.

Didn't I know it? Here was a black man very much like me, with pride and talent—a three-time all-star, seven-time Gold Glove winner, a career batting average .298—complaining about major league baseball's injustices. A federal court in New York ruled against Curt, saying the reserve clause was needed to keep the major league teams balanced and no one team could get all the best players. Curt finally appealed to the Supreme Court, which upheld the lower court's ruling in 1971.

A brief player's strike in 1972 and the threat of one in '73 led to the reserve clause being amended: If a player had ten years of major leagues experience, the last five with the same club, he couldn't be traded without his consent. And if there was a dispute about salaries, an arbitrator would be brought in. But even those concessions weren't good enough. In 1975, Andy Messersmith of the Los Angeles Dodgers and Dave McNally of the Montreal Expos went to a three-man arbitration board, which struck down the reserve clause. Right after that, big money started rolling in for ballplayers. But all the credit goes to Curt, who passed away in January 1997. He had the gumption to challenge the century-old clause. And when today's players get paid, they should always remember that if it weren't for Curt, they wouldn't have all those zeros in their paychecks.

As soon as I got my release in 1955, the Licey team from the Dominican Republican called and asked me to play for them. I didn't mind going back there, but I wasn't going alone. I told them my wife was sick and I didn't want to leave her. "Come on down and bring her with you," they told me. That was just fine. Sadie and little Michael joined me there.

Funny thing was I got to play in the first game in that brand new stadium, the one that forced the league to shut down two years prior. And that trip to the Dominican Republic sticks out for Sadie too. One day a friend hailed down what she thought was a cab for Sadie. The car pulled over and Sadie jumped right on in. They drove for about eight blocks and the driver started talking to her about this and that. When they reached their destination, Sadie reached into her pocket to pay him.

"How much do I owe you?" she asked.

"Nothing," the driver said. "I'm a doctor, not a cab driver." Well, Sadie just about fell out laughing.

On December 26, 1955, I watched Charlie Neal, who would go on to become second baseman for the Dodgers, set a record for triples hit in a season down there. He popped seven in two months.

I didn't know it then, but that game would be my last.

Mr. Wickland's antics had pushed me over the edge. Even though I had gotten my release, I was tired of playing mind games, of having promises made to me only to be broken later, and of being a man of honor among so many dishonorable men. I had a family that loved me and missed me.

I was thirty-six years old, and even though I felt I could play at least four more years, I had to ask myself: Was it worth it?

I knew the answer.

I hung up my spikes.

CHAPTER 11

SLIDING HOME

✻ ✻ ✻

The man who views the world at 50 the same as he did at 20 has wasted 30 years of his life.
—Muhammad Ali

When I retired from baseball, I had plenty of things to take up my time. I had left the Lester Piano Company and worked a few months in a machine shop at New York Shipbuilding Corp. in Camden, New Jersey, before returning to Westinghouse. I could finally watch my kids Billy, Janet, and Michael grow up without interruption.

But around the country, black people were getting restless. Black leaders continued to push for equality, civil rights, and the end of discrimination. They saw fourteen-year-old Emmett Till kidnapped and lynched because white folks said he allegedly made some comment to a white woman. They saw Rosa Parks, a passenger on a bus in Montgomery, Alabama, arrested because she didn't feel like getting out of her seat so a white man could sit down. And though in 1954, the Supreme Court ordered schools integrated "with all deliberate speed," stubborn school board leaders moved slow as molasses—or not at all—to carry out the order.

The Rev. Dr. Martin Luther King preached non-violence and equality and did a good job. Now that man was something else. I was so moved by his message that I went to Washington, D.C., on August 28, 1963, participated in the most famous civil rights march, and heard the most famous civil rights speech ever delivered.

One of the unions at Westinghouse chartered seven buses to travel to Washington. Called the "March on Washington for Jobs and Freedom," it had stirred interest from all kinds of people who wanted to right the wrongs of this country. Black, white, Jewish people, Christian people, union supporters—everybody felt the pull of this march.

So two hundred fifty thousand of us from across the country got on buses, trains, carpooled, walked, did whatever to get there on that hot day, and gathered in front of the Lincoln Memorial. That's when we heard the great speeches by John Lewis of the Student Nonviolent Coordinating Committee and others.

But it was King's "I Have a Dream" speech that really hit a home run with us and the rest of the nation. To be honest, I didn't know at the time it would turn into such a famous speech, but I knew he had said something special. I came home rejuvenated and hopeful that things would change for us.

But by the mid-1960s, black people in northern cities just got plain old fed up. Marching wasn't working. They took to rioting.

In 1964, Philadelphia was one of several cities where black folk took to the streets. That August, there had already been riots in Harlem, as well as in a suburb of Chicago and three cities in New Jersey—Jersey City, Paterson, and Elizabeth.

Columbia Avenue in North Philadelphia used to be called "Jump Street" because so much jumped off there. You had your jazz clubs, theaters, hardware stores, restaurants, meat shops, and bars. It was a great entertainment and business strip for black Philadelphians.

But on August 28, an argument between Odessa Bradford and her husband, Rush, in a car stopped in the intersection of Twenty-second and Columbia brought the cops. And the thing is the first cop on the scene, Robert Wells, was black. Philadelphia had done a better job than most cities at integrating its police force. According to newspaper accounts, Wells told the Bradfords to move the car. Words and slaps were exchanged between a drunk Odessa Bradford and Wells.

"Me and my big mouth," Bradford told the *Philadelphia Inquirer* twenty-five years after the riot. "I'll be honest, I was blasted."

While Wells was putting Bradford in the paddy wagon, a white cop, John Hoff, held the door. A man came out of the crowd that had gathered and punched Hoff in the head. The same man went after Wells. Then all hell broke loose.

See, the riot was fueled in part by rumors that police had shot or beaten a pregnant woman and that they had shot and killed a young boy. It lasted two days. One person died, three hundred forty were injured, including one hundred cops. Of the six hundred rioters taken into custody, three hundred ten were charged. Estimates are that six hundred businesses were damaged at a cost of $3 million. But it could've been far worse, if not for the city's black leadership—Cecil B. Moore, then head of the

NAACP, and WDAS-AM radio personality Georgie Woods ("The Guy with the Goods") among others—and Police Commissioner Howard R. Leary, who kept his men from getting too aggressive and kept the rioters boxed in.

Man, that riot destroyed Columbia Avenue. For years it was the city's symbol of urban blight. Now the city is trying to restore Columbia Avenue to some of its former grandeur with new construction projects. And it has been renamed Cecil B. Moore Avenue.

People walk and mingle on debris-strewn Columbia Avenue in North Philadelphia in the aftermath of the 1964 riots. (Credit: Temple University Libraries, Urban Archives, Philadelphia, Pa.)

But what happened in Philly couldn't compare to what occurred later in Newark, Cleveland, Detroit, and Los Angeles.

The Watts riots stick with me. In 1965, I had a chance to return to beautiful Canada. Sadie, Michael, and I took a two-week vacation up there and eventually stopped in Granby to visit Ramone Forand and his family. Even after fifteen years, Granby was still pleasant and peaceful.

We went to Ramone's lakeside cabin. And I remember I nearly drowned trying to swim from a buoy to the shore with one of Ramone's sons. Shoot, I hadn't swum in years, and after a few seconds, my legs turned to lead. Don't ask me, I don't know what I was trying to prove. They brought a motor boat alongside of us and we hung to it while it towed us to shore.

But what happened after we returned to the cabin is what stands out about that vacation. We turned on the television, and there were scenes from the Watts riots. It seemed so odd. Here we were, a Negro family from Philadelphia, feeling at home and comfortable with white people from Canada who had treated us with nothing but compassion and respect. And there flickering on the screen were angry black people from a poor, rundown part of Los Angeles, looting, setting fires, throwing stones and bottles at the white cops and firefighters. They were filled with rage built by years of poverty and overcrowding.

Ramone turned to me and said, "We don't have that here."

I had to agree. "We sure don't." But I knew their frustration, the prejudice they felt. I knew they were fighting for survival.

According to reports, the whole thing was sparked by the arrest of a young black man in the early evening of August 11 on suspicion of drunken driving. The residents of Watts apparently resented the white police force—seemed like they pulled over more black people than white. It was hot. A crowd gathered and grew. There were rumors of police brutality, and then things went crazy. It was time to get "whitey."

After a few days, the National Guard was called in. The local cops couldn't handle the bands of resident rebels. The Guard set up machine guns at street intersections and built roadblocks. Curfews were enforced.

Thankfully it was over after six days. Most people agree Watts looked like a smoldering war zone afterward. Reports of the incident said thirty-four people died, more than one thousand were injured, and four thousand arrested. The riots caused $35 million in property damage.

I just shake my head when I look back at that era. Sure, some gains were made by black people, but at the cost of a lot of pain.

With extra time on my hands, I helped start a Little League team in my neighborhood. Bob Bembry (whose dad coached me on the Liberty Stars), his wife, Roberta, and some other parents decided to start a league after a couple of kids who lived at Sixty-first and Carpenter streets were accepted to play on the local PAL baseball team but wound up riding the bench. Bob called it a case "of color and hoodlums"—the Elmwood kids were black, but they weren't hoods, so they didn't get to play. Most of the PAL kids, Bob said, were troublemakers.

So he got the paperwork from the Little League headquarters and asked me to help out. I was glad to do it. And in 1970, the Parkway Little League was born for kids nine to twelve years old. We had four teams that played in hand-me-down uniforms given to us by a white organization from Haddon Heights, New Jersey. The Parkway Little League lasted until 1975.

The kids who played in that league got respect from neighborhood thugs. Bob told the story that one day he saw a gang about to pounce on one of our Little League players. But suddenly one gang member stopped them. "We can't fight him," the gang member said. "He's a Little Leaguer."

We both got a chuckle out of that. And many of the kids involved in that Little League would go on to become good citizens. In fact, Bob's son, Bob III, is now a lawyer. I believed in kids and baseball so strongly that I reorganized the league in 1986 and called it the Cobbs Creek Little League.

With my free time, I also did some umpiring—I called the last game played between Philadelphia's public league and Catholic league champions at Veterans Stadium—and in more recent years have been active with several Negro League players' associations. I wasn't like some retired ballplayers, who get bored with being home, who miss life on the road, and who think they could still play if given the chance.

I still follow all sports—basketball, football, you name it. I love to read about them in magazines and newspapers and watch them on television. Some days, when I'm really feeling energetic, I think I would like to be a baseball scout whose territory would be the Dominican Republic. Oh, man, what a nice thought. That's a hot area nowadays, and major league baseball is finally getting the message that there are a huge number of talented Latin ballplayers available.

I retired from Westinghouse February 1, 1985, after putting in thirty years at the plant. I would've stayed until April, but things were getting crazy there—people getting fired for no reason, that kind of stuff. Rather than risk being fired and losing my pension, I got out early. Sixty-eight of us retired that day. I have never looked back.

Most fathers like to say they didn't try to influence what their kids do for a living. But when you see an offspring with talent, it's hard to stay out of the way, if you know what I mean.

Billy had that talent. I don't know if it came from watching the old man play the game in all those different countries and states or what, but the kid could play ball. When I was in the White Sox organization, I had taught him how to play first base, the outfield, and pitch.

One day when he was about twelve, Billy was out on the field playing first base while we were warming up. The guys were throwing the ball into the dirt, and Billy was scooping them up like it was nothing. One of the Chicago scouts sent to check me out—I was recuperating from a broken leg and they wanted to know how I was doing—jokingly asked me if I wanted to sell Bill. "He's not ready yet," I said, laughing.

Then one of my teammates, Walt Millies, chimed in. "What the hell do you care whether he's ready or not? Sell him!"

Funny thing was Billy wasn't a catcher. He wound up pitching and playing first base. I worked with Billy on his pitching. He was a lefty, and I used to have him throw to me, using a case quarter as home plate. I taught him the fundamentals: the importance of a follow-through, of keeping your eye on the catcher's mitt, and using the triangle created by the catcher's mitt and knees as a target.

In his sophomore year at Bok Vocational and Technical High School, Billy tried out for the baseball team at first base. The kid trying out at third kept throwing the ball way over Billy's head, making him look bad. Billy didn't make the roster, but a year later he was on the team as a pitcher.

And he was Bok's best pitcher. One year Bok won only six games—Billy was responsible for five of them. In his senior year, in a game against South Philadelphia High School, Billy struck out seventeen men, but lost 16-1 or something like that. He had no defensive support. I remember one game he pitched a one-hitter and they still lost.

I used to help the team out every now and then, working with the outfielders, hitting them fly balls and stuff. But the coach didn't know nothing about baseball. I mean the little things, like when to hit and run, when to bunt, when to sacrifice.

It didn't matter to Billy; he wanted to play ball. I told him, "Get your education. If you want to go to college, we'll see that you go to college."

But Billy wasn't interested in college. "I want to be a ballplayer," he told me.

In 1960, I talked to William McKechnie, former manager of the Cincinnati Reds (1938–1946), whose son was a Reds farm team director. McKechnie's son told me Billy would have to pay his way down to Tampa, Florida, for a tryout, and if he was signed, he would be reimbursed. That was all Billy needed to hear. He had a great-aunt in Tampa and could stay with her. We gave him the money for the trip.

He was there thirty days and had Johnny Vandermere, a star pitcher for the 1938 Reds, as his coach. Billy pitched one batting practice and nobody could hit him. The Reds said they liked him but were worried about his age and the possibility of him getting drafted. They told Billy that if they signed him to a contract and he was drafted, they would still have to pay him. They told him to take care of his military obligations first then come back and see them.

There was no real war going on. Sure, the cold war with Russia was heating up, but looking back on it now, Billy thinks the Reds' reasoning was a bunch of bull.

But when Bill returned home to us, he was fired up. He wanted to sign up for the military right away. He wanted to go into the air force. I told him that "whatever you do, learn something you can use when you get out of the service."

Billy wanted to be an electronics technician. That sounded impressive and all, but Billy couldn't tell you the difference between AC and DC to save his life. He went to the air force recruiting station to take his test. And I didn't realize until later that whatever profession the air force was looking for on the day the test was taken, that's what the applicants somehow wound up being good at. That day it was communications. Billy was snatched up that same day and shipped to Texas. And when he came back from boot camp, he could out-type anybody. He was given the title of intelligence officer.

Then a funny thing happened. One day, two big guys—one black and one white—stopped by the house

and started asking tough questions. When did Billy
go out of the country? Why didn't he have a passport?
These guys were checking into Billy's background. Well,
it turned out the black guy was a cousin of Bus Clarkson,
who was captain of the Stars when I played. And after
I explained they had me confused with my son, the
black guy put his pen down and just started asking me
questions about the Negro Leagues.

Billy went to Wiesbaden, Germany. He stayed there
about ten months on an army post waiting for top-secret
clearance. Now Billy could draw, and with a talent for
commercial art, he spent his time away by making an
air force squadron sign and decorating the air force
squadron day room.

When volunteers were needed to go to a new Royal
Air Force communications center in Great Britain, Billy
was one of the first to sign up. This also gave him a
chance to again play baseball.

He played first base and pitched. His team won
second place in the country's air force league. But in
the fifth or sixth inning of one game, some guy fouled
off a half-dozen of his pitches. Now Billy had this nasty
sinker he sometimes threw. To the batter, it looked like
the ball just slipped out of his hand, but it would break
wickedly over the plate. Well, Billy threw it and felt
pins shoot through his arm and elbow. He had pulled
ligaments in his elbow. He's not sure why it happened.
Maybe he hadn't warmed up long enough on that cool
day. Maybe he took his jacket off too soon. Who knows?

I always told him, "Never change your style of
pitching because your muscles are acclimated to the
way you throw, and if you do change, you're going to
screw things up."

But Billy was never the same. He tried to throw before the season was over, but it was no use. He gave up sports when he came home in September 1963, and after doing some commercial artwork for a lamp company, joined the Philadelphia Police Department in July 1965.

He put in twenty-eight-and-a-half years with the Philadelphia Police Department, seventeen in the District Attorney's office. And he's retired from the Air Force Reserves. He says that when he turns sixty-five, he'll have four checks coming in: from the police department, Social Security, the state, and the Air Force Reserves. Shoot, by that time, he can slip his old man a couple of bucks.

Billy lives in the Mount Airy section of Philadelphia. Like me, he's disturbed by today's ballplayers and pitchers who can't throw strikes. (Billy was a big fan of Sandy Koufax.) Billy doesn't watch much baseball these days because it's not interesting.

Michael, my youngest, didn't have much interest in baseball. He played a little playground basketball, but nothing too serious. Mike was a rambunctious and rebellious kid. Seemed like he was against anything I said.

I should've known he was going to be a fighter. I remember when Sadie and I took him to the Dominican Republic in the 1955 winter season. Mike was about two years old, and we had him dressed in a cute little suit with a coat and cap. Well, the young kids down there didn't dress quite like that. The boys usually wore only shirts and no pants, the girls just wore panties. When they saw Mike, they thought he was strange. "Look, look, look," they said in Spanish while pointing at him. Even at two, Mike didn't take any stuff. He started swinging at the kids, hitting their fingers with his little fists.

But he turned out to be a good kid. Today he oversees the Delaware River Port Authority toll plaza at the Walt Whitman Bridge, which spans the Delaware River between Philadelphia and Gloucester City, New Jersey.

As for my daughter, Janet, well, she went through it. At thirty-five, she was diagnosed with breast cancer and had a mastectomy. But she didn't take things sitting down. She became very active in promoting breast cancer awareness, especially for black women. She won several awards for her advocacy, led a workshop in Beijing on African American women and breast cancer, and even co-founded a breast awareness program called "Sisters in Touch." Sadly, my beautiful daughter, who was one of my biggest supporters, died of pneumonia on September 25, 2010. She was sixty-six.

My own father lived to be ninety-seven. He didn't get baptized until he was ninety-three. And when he emerged from the baptism pool, I was there and hugged him. When we were young, he would take the family to church but wouldn't stay. He said he used to belong to a church in Georgia, where he got a foot wash baptism, but never bothered to get baptized up north until we started attending a church in West Philadelphia. I'm not sure why Pop finally decided to become a Christian at such a late age, but I thank God that he did.

Pop died right here on our dining room floor in 1990. He was living with us because Mom had died December 26, 1984, right on their seventy-second wedding anniversary. She was ninety-three and had

Alzheimer's disease real bad. It was a blessing for that sweet woman to pass.

And my brothers? Well, unfortunately they all took to the bottle. They drank like fish and died early. Sometimes Joe would get so drunk, he would fall into the gutter. Two years before Joe died, the doctor told him to stop drinking or else he'd get cirrhosis of the liver. Now Joe had a wife, Julia, at home, but he would go over to his girlfriend's house and get to drinking.

One day before Christmas, after finishing my midnight to 8 a.m. shift at Westinghouse, I met Joe at the bank on Fifty-eighth and Baltimore. He had this big old patch on the side of his head. "I was up on a ladder hanging curtains for Julia," Joe said. "I fell and hit my head on the corner of the ladder. I've got to go to the hospital this afternoon."

I said I'd drive him to the Physicians and Surgeons Hospital at Seventeenth and Green streets. Public transportation didn't run up there regularly. I told him to give me a call when he was ready.

I went home and went to bed. Around 7:30 p.m., my father called. Joe had made it to the hospital but fell in the hospital bathroom. A doctor pronounced him dead right there. Just like the doctor warned, Joe died of cirrhosis.

Arthur, who suffered from lung problems because he'd sandblast without a mask, died in his sleep in 1964 after drinking heavily while on a weekend pass from the hospital. Back in those days, they often sent people with respiratory problems to the mountains. But the doctors treating Arthur thought he'd make out better if he was kept at the Landis Hospital at Twenty-fifth and Girard Avenue, which specialized in treating people suffering from tuberculosis. Arthur had a spot on his right lung, but his left lung was clear. They told him not to drink. Arthur liked his beer.

Arthur spent two-and-a-half years in the hospital. One forty-eight-hour period was his undoing. He and Joe got together and started drinking Friday afternoon and Friday night. On Saturday morning they went over to Tip's house, which was right across the street from a state liquor store, and drank all day and night. On Sunday morning Arthur stumbled back to the hospital and fell asleep. He never woke up. The booze and his medication to heal his respiratory problems didn't mix.

The doctors wanted to perform an autopsy on Arthur, to be absolutely sure of why he died and perhaps learn something that could one day help them help another patient. Pop refused. He didn't want anyone slicing up his son's body. The doctors pressed the issue, but Pop stood firm. Just to be sure, I utilized a Mason connection. The undertaker was a member of my lodge. "If they cut my brother," I told the undertaker, "I want to know it."

There was no autopsy.

Arthur's life insurance, five thousand seven hundred dollars, went to Mom. She had dreamed of a new dining room set, but for years my pop said they didn't need one. Mom never asked for much. But she took that insurance money and bought herself a beautiful dining room set. And when she passed, I gave the set to Michael. It's still in great shape.

Tip was one of the best crane operators in Westinghouse, even when he was drunk. One of his bosses told me he'd rather have Tip half-drunk operating a fifty-ton crane than any sober white man.

Tip would go to work so drunk that I was amazed he could climb up the crane's ladder. But he also had people looking out for him. Art, a fellow crane operator, was crazy about Tip. If he saw Tip was in really bad shape, he'd push Tip's crane down the far end of the yard and told the supervisors that if they needed a lift, call him.

I remember the day Tip died. He was already in the hospital, suffering from throat cancer that had been made worse by his drinking. He was on life support, and the doctor told his wife, Helen, that if Tip came to, he would be nothing but a vegetable. Helen wasn't sure what to do. She asked me for advice, since I was the closest member of his immediate family.

"Helen, that's your husband. Whatever decision you make, I'll go with it."

They took Tip off life support that day. He died a few hours later.

Me? I never was a drinker. I don't know why. It just never appealed to me. My brothers used to tease me, called me "goody-goody" because I went to church, stayed away from the booze, and didn't run around. It's hard to explain why I walked the straight and narrow. When we were younger, we all went to church. In fact, I still remember how, back in Round Oak, Mom took us one-and-a-half miles through creeks and what-have-you to get to church. Sometimes we heard the Baptist congregation singing before we got there, and that's when Mom hurried us along. So we all had the same chance to learn right from wrong. I guess it just took with me.

My own kids say I was a no-nonsense dad. Billy called me the toughest father around. Michael likes to say I was "strict but fair." And I was. Some of that I got from my own pop. Some of it was because I saw how the kids were in the neighborhood. They were getting into fights and killing each other over nonsense. I remember a kid named Arthur Fields was cut to death by William Ash because Ash had lost money in a crap game Christmas Day one year.

I was really serious about teaching Billy, Janet, and Michael about responsibility—taking out trash, cleaning up around the house. It wasn't so much that I was trying to be mean. I was just preparing them for adulthood. I remember how as a kid, I got firewood ready at night, then at five in the morning made the fire in our stove so my mother could cook biscuits and a full-course meal for my father before he left for work. I remember making the beds, having the newspaper route, leaving school early to help the household, getting my brothers to pitch in so Mom could stop scrubbing floors. That was how I learned responsibility.

Michael now says he's grateful I stayed on them. "It made a better person out of all of us," he says.

My day-to-day activities center around three things. Home, church (I'm a member of and a deacon at the First African Baptist Church of Darby Township, Pennsylvania, where the Rev. Dr. Richard A. Dent is pastor), and the Masons.

Funny what can get you interested in something. For me and the Masons, it was watching members of the local lodge march from their hall to Eighty-sixth and Eastwick as part of a cornerstone laying ceremony in 1950. I already had some cousins and two uncles in the Prince Hall Masons, whose history dates back to the late 1700s.

This group of men was special, and the more I heard about them—their fight against slavery, their work in the civil rights movement, and their efforts to improve the status of blacks—the more I wanted to belong.

There are white masons and black masons. We black masons are officially known as the Prince Hall Freemasons. We share the same ideas, and our structure is similar to the white group, but we ran into the same problems as we did with baseball—whites wanted to keep blacks out of their social lives. Prince Hall Freemasonry is sort of like the Negro Leagues, only it's much stronger and has lasted much longer.

Prince Hall Masons came about because the white American masons, who came over from Britain in the late 1700s and settled in the Boston area, didn't want blacks to join. A British Army lodge finally let a free black Methodist minister named Prince Hall and a few other blacks join its lodge. Eventually Hall started African Lodge 456 in Boston, but the American Masons wouldn't accept their charter. Hall's group had to get its charter from the Grand Lodge of England. The American Prince Hall Grand Lodge was established in 1791.

I was admitted into the Light of Elmwood Lodge #45, Free and Accepted Masons, in 1951, along with Walter Alexander and Mack Meens. During my last year with the Stars, I studied my Masonry manuals while we were on the road. This was mostly a lonely practice because there were no other Masons on the team. In fact, in all the years I played in the Negro Leagues, I never knew of one player who was a Mason. Now I'm not saying there weren't any, but I sure didn't know of them.

I got my third degree in September 1953. Masons have thirty-three degrees, and getting the third gets you on the road to sovereign grand inspector general, the top rank in Masonry. And to show you how far Masonry reaches, I attended a lodge in the Dominican Republic while playing ball there.

Once I quit baseball, Rodgers A. Hope, the master of the local lodge, really got me involved. Then another member, John Nelson, asked me to do a historical tract for the lodge.

I've held several offices, including past master (I'm the oldest active past member in the lodge). I'm also a Shriner. In order to be a Shriner, you have to be a thirty-second- or thirty-third-degree Mason or Knight Templar. I'm a thirty-third-degree Mason myself. And I'm still active to this day. To me, being a Mason and Shriner isn't an ego thing. The greatest satisfaction I get is my knowing that I've served my fellow man.

But the people who could care less about their fellow men were the politicians of Philadelphia in the late 1950s. They came up with this brilliant plan to knock down my neighborhood. I got to tell you about this, because it hurt me so much.

See, Elmwood was a beautiful place, a melting pot of different races and religions sprawled out among wide-open farmland. Maybe the neighborhood was too much of a good thing, for the politicians were licking their lips to do something to it. Their idea?

Redevelopment.

In those days, redevelopment seemed to be the cure for all city problems. It meant getting government money, an increased tax base, a chance for political big shots to create new houses to soothe their egos, and a chance for redevelopers to make big bucks. Forget about the people who live there.

The redevelopment of Elmwood officially started in 1958. Residents like me and Sadie were told we had to move because of "progress," and if you didn't buy that, the city used the term "eminent domain" to frighten you. Many of the houses were in fine condition, but the politicians claimed they weren't. And when the city bought the houses from residents, they often offered much less money than the house was worth.

Our neighborhood was near the airport. What better spot to put up a brand new community with houses, offices complexes, strip malls, and hotels, they thought. Despite protests, the city uprooted nearly ten thousand people. Many long-time residents couldn't take the change. Some became sick. Some, I'm told, were so upset they died. Shoot, being forced to move, especially under those circumstances, isn't pleasant.

Sadie, the kids, and I had to move too. We weren't happy. Our house was wonderful with a seventy-five-foot by 120-foot front yard for the kids, a two-car garage, everything. But we found a corner house in West Philadelphia with a basement that could be entered from the sidewalk. Sadie, who by the way has a degree in cosmetology, set up her beauty shop down there.

Former Elmwood residents hold a reunion picnic every year in the old neighborhood to renew acquaintances and recall those great days. I haven't been to one of those picnics, but I've heard stories about them and even watched videotape of one.

No matter how many reunions are held, they can never recapture the loving atmosphere of our neighborhood United Nations.

CHAPTER 12

OH, AND ANOTHER THING...

* * *

*Since baseball time is measured only in outs, all you
have to do is succeed utterly; keep hitting, keep the rally
alive, and you have defeated time. You remain forever
young.*

—Baseball writer Roger Angell

I didn't get misty-eyed or heartbroken when I decided
to stop playing baseball. And there's still some talk
that when I protested that call back in '46 and
accidentally smacked the ump, I ruined any chance of
playing major league baseball. I don't know. But no one
can doubt my love for the game.

When I look at today's ballplayers, I just have to
shake my head. Now I'm not bitter about the money
they're pulling in, but I question their work ethnic. They
don't have the dedication to the game we had. I mean,
any little thing comes along and they're ready to take a
day off. In my time, playing with broken bones wasn't
unusual. If the good Lord decided to take away my age
and return my abilities—I admit that my knees crack
every now and then—I'd love to be back on the field
with those youngsters. I'd show them a thing or two.

To be a good catcher, you have to be knowledgeable.
And that's missing in a lot of today's players. Don't get

me wrong. There are a few catchers in major league baseball these days that do a good job. But some catchers don't have the fundamentals right. I mean, you should know how to position your body to throw out a base stealer. If the ball is pitched outside on a right-handed batter, you just don't stand up and throw the ball to second base. You take a step with your right foot, plant and put all your weight behind the throw. That's how you get humph on that ball.

But baseball has a long way to go to bring the fans back to the game. You know, fans don't like seeing all that money going to ballplayers and not getting anything back. The players don't seem to get the fundamentals right. They don't even know how to throw behind a runner, for gosh sakes.

Major league baseball didn't help its cause by expanding so fast, either. The talent has become so diluted that teams have to bring up Class A players to fill their rosters. And when it comes to starting pitchers, man, do we have a problem. The excitement has been diluted too. When I played, base stealing and bunting hits were automatic parts of the game. Now, it's just done in certain situations at certain times in the game. There was nothing as exciting as the battle between a base runner and a good catcher. Will he make it to second? Will the throw be on the money or high? Everyone, including the fans, had to pay attention and be ready for anything.

Another problem with major league baseball these days: The players can get away with just about any bad conduct on or off the field. Instead of expecting the commissioner of baseball to be responsible for these things, maybe team owners should have the responsibility of handling discipline and drug problems. The players also have to stop being big babies and start carrying themselves with dignity and respect. They should be impeccable, and if you stay on the straight and narrow and believe in the Lord, that's not so hard to do.

Baseball could use some other help: They have to speed up the game. A three-and-a-half-hour baseball game is crazy. As much as I love baseball, even I wouldn't want to play in a game that long. I know they don't want to tinker with tradition, but we live in a faster era now. We eat at fast-food restaurants. We cook our meals in microwave ovens. We can fly to Europe in just four or five hours.

So baseball needs to speed up. The first place to start is with those darn pitchers. Even in my day, I couldn't understand why some pitchers took so dang long to throw me the pill. Just get my signal and throw it. Simple enough. Batters aren't off the hook, either. Remember when Lenny Dykstra played? When he was up to bat, he would step out of the batter's box after every single pitch. Then he had to do his housekeeping: Pull up his batting gloves, fix his hat, scrape away some dirt around home plate. Lenny was an idol to thousands of kids, and when they saw him tug and pull and spit and just act all finicky outside the batter's box, they wanted to do the same thing. The cycle will never end.

My solution: call strikes even when the batter's out of the box. That'll teach them.

Now Philadelphia is my hometown and I love it dearly. I have great memories here. A lot of people ask me about the Phillies. You know, do I follow them? What do I think of them?

Well, I didn't like them for a long, long time. But they've grown on me.

My bitterness was based on history and the way the Phillies used to treat black players. I didn't start out disliking them; shoot, I even wanted to play for them once. It was around 1947 or so, just when they started to seriously take Negro League players. I went down to see Herb Pennock, the Phillies general manager, about giving me a shot. He knew what I could do. He had seen me play with the Stars on Mondays at Shibe Park. Robert Carpenter Sr. was the team owner, but he let his son, Bob Jr., run things as club president.

"Mr. Carpenter is trying to build a championship team," Pennock told me. "Meantime I'm gonna give you a tryout."

Well, wouldn't you know it? In January 1948, Pennock went to New York for a league meeting, reached for the door, and dropped dead from a heart attack. Bob Jr. took over his duties and I never heard another thing about playing for the Phillies.

Like I said, it wasn't just one incident. The Phillies were the last team in the National League to integrate. That seems to be way things went in Philadelphia baseball history. I heard that in the late '20s and early '30s, another Philadelphia icon had problems with race.

Connie Mack, legendary manager of the Philadelphia A's, was asked whether he would put blacks on his team. He said no because then there wouldn't be any place on the team for white players. I guess that was a backhanded compliment. When Mack took his "world champions" to play the Hilldale baseball club, they lost. In fact, Phil Cocker, one of Hilldale's pitchers, told me they used to shut them out nearly all the time. And this became too much for Commissioner Kenesaw "Mountain" Landis who, in 1923, stopped white professional teams from playing black teams. He hated the idea that a bunch of black men could beat his guys. They wouldn't officially play another black team until 1935, when Dizzy Dean had a group of white all-stars play Satchel Paige's all-stars. That's when Dizzy called Satchel the greatest pitcher that ever lived. By the way, Dizzy's group lost.

Also, the Phillies had a chance to get Campy, but they didn't want him.

The Phillies didn't sign a black ballplayer until 1957, ten years after the Dodgers signed Jackie. That was infielder John Kennedy of the Birmingham Black Barons. John played only five games for the Phillies. But years later in Jacksonville, Florida, when he was in his late fifties, John joined a thirty-and-over league and played until he was seventy. That guy never stopped loving the game. He died in 1998.

This view of the Phillies wasn't mine alone. In a November 1998 column, Paul Hagen, baseball writer for the *Philadelphia Daily News*, wrote:

"Even if the Phillies' won-lost record doesn't improve in 1999, they have at least made great strides in erasing the perception that they have ignored African-American talent over the years.

"In the fifth game of the 1996 season, then manager Jim Fregosi started an all-white lineup. In July, when outfielder Glenn Murray went on the disabled list, the Phillies didn't have a single U.S.-born black on the active roster."

And look at what they did to Dick Allen.

In 1964, Dick was named Rookie of the Year for the Phillies, playing third base and hitting the ball like nobody's business. Before making the major leagues, he was the first black player to play for the Arkansas Travelers in Little Rock, Arkansas. The Travelers were a Triple A club that the Phils had just taken over in '63.

Dick caught heck in Little Rock. Some "fans" called him "Chocolate Drop." Cops stopped him while he was jogging and carrying a soda from a vending machine. Some folks left death threats on his car windshield. Gun shots made him jumpy. But Dick didn't talk about these bad experiences to many people. In fact, he pulled back from people, especially sports writers and scouts who saw his standoffish attitude as negative. But they didn't understand. Like I said before, you have to know where a person comes from to understand why he acts the way he does.

So Dick played angry and was tagged as a "rebel," a label he couldn't shed. And then there was that Frank Thomas incident in 1965. It was batting practice, and Dick was taking ground balls at third when John Callison came over. They decided to tease Thomas a little. The night before, the big slugger had tried to bunt with men on first and third and one out.

According to Dick's book *Crash*, Callison hollered, "Why don't you try to bunt instead?"

Well, Thomas knew it was Callison yelling at him, but he directed his anger at Dick. "What are you trying to be, another Muhammad Clay, always running your mouth off?"

Dick went to the batting cage and punched Thomas in the jaw. Thomas hit him in the shoulder with a baseball bat.

Want to know why Dick had "an attitude?" Imagine shopping with your wife and three kids—and folks spitting on you. Imagine coming home and finding your lawn messed up by tire tracks and your house windows broken. But everyday fans didn't know about these things. We Negro Leaguers found out about them from one of Dick's brothers. Any man, given those circumstances, would be upset and leery. Phillies management and fans didn't care. He just wasn't being a good Negro.

Amazingly, Dick has managed to put that stuff behind him. And he's now community relations representative for the Phillies.

Yes, things have really changed. Now the team is lead by two talented black men, shortstop Jimmy Rollins, who made the club in 2000, and slugger Ryan Howard, who came on board in 2005. I consider both of them my buddies. They were crucial to the Phillies winning the 2008 World Series (that Phillies team really played together; if one guy didn't get it done at the plate, the next guy would come up and take care of business. And Brad Lidge, the Phillies closer? He had his stuff with him back then) and helped make the Phillies one of the best teams in baseball over the past four years.

Phillies superstar Ryan Howard with Bill and teammate Mahlon Ducket at the 103rd Philadelphia Sports Writers Association Annual Awards Dinner in 2007. Howard received the association's Outstanding Professional Athlete Award. (Credit: Yong Kim, Philadelphia Daily News.)

But over the last few years, the Phillies have really reached out to us Negro Leaguers, inviting us to special events and highlighting us on Jackie Robinson Day. They dedicated the Negro League Pavilion in Philadelphia's Veterans Stadium in 1996. In June 2003, the other surviving Stars and I went to Veterans Stadium (which was demolished in March 2004) to attend the unveiling of a statue sculpted by artist Phil Sumpter that honors us. It's seven feet tall, weighs about one thousand pounds, and is made out of bronze. It's now in the Negro League Memorial Park,

Forty-fourth and Parkside Avenue, where we played our home games. And in 2008, the Phillies "drafted" Duckett during a Major League Baseball ceremony that acknowledged Negro League players who didn't get to play with a major league team or organization. The Phillies, however, also recognized me and Glenn as ceremonial draft picks during a special event at the team's new ballpark, Citizens Bank Park. Another Philadelphia Star, Harold Gould, was selected by the Toronto Blue Jays.

The effort by Major League Baseball and the Phillies to include us seems genuine, so I'm not as bitter as I once was.

Public interest in the Negro Leagues and their players seemed to grow in 1979, when Schlitz Beer Company sponsored a reunion of Negro League players down in Greenup, Kentucky, just outside Ashland. It started out with a birthday party for Clint Thomas, a former outfielder with the Detroit Stars and a few other teams. About ten Negro Leaguers went down to honor him. Benson was one of the guys who went. Also there were Buck Leonard, Lorenzo "Piper" Davis, Sam "The Jet" Jethroe, Judy Johnson, Quincy Trouppe, and Othello "Chico" Renfroe. A reporter had those guys over to his house, fed them, and told their story in the paper. Word got out that these players had gathered, and that's when Schlitz got on board. Every year they would bring different players down. I went in 1980, when thirty of us showed up, then in '81, '82, and '83, when about sixty of us came.

We had a good old time renewing old times with the fellas, like Quincy, Judy, Buck, and Ray Dandridge. I remember the 1982 gathering real well because that was the last time I got to talk to Satch before he died. And Sadie had a good talk with his wife, Lahoma Jean.

Satch was in a wheelchair. He suffered from emphysema and had to use portable oxygen to help him breathe. But while I was talking to him, he kept pulling out the oxygen tubes from his nose.

"Satch, you better put that back in your nose."

He said, "Man, I can't breathe with that thing in my nose!"

We just talked about baseball for about ninety minutes. Satch was still a little teed off that the American League banned his legendary hesitation pitch when he broke into the majors as a "rookie" in 1948. He had such elasticity in his arm that he could rare up his foot, plant it down, and then throw. We saw this all the time in the Negro Leagues, so we were used to it. But the newfangled motion messed up the timing of the white hitters, who started swinging when Satch planted his foot. So they banned it.

Anyway, the good-time reunions didn't last very long. Coors bought Schlitz in '83 and decided to stop sponsoring them.

That was OK. My daughter Janet did something special for me in 1985. She worked her head off putting together a program to honor me and my contribution to the Negro Leagues. People came from all over the country to the Adams Mark Hotel on City Avenue in Philadelphia on April 9, 1985. The turnout was wonderful. A television news crew recorded the event.

In 1989, the Atlanta Braves and Southern Bell invited about eighty of us Negro Leaguers down for a reunion. This came about thanks to the hard work of Chico, who himself was honored in 1987 by Morris Brown College at the Hyatt Regency in Atlanta, and then convinced the Braves and Southern Bell to sponsor the '89 reunion. It also helped that Chico was close to the Braves' Hank Aaron and knew the vice president of Southern Bell.

There were players there from the '30s and '40s, and we were dubbed the "Black Legends of Baseball." Pretty impressive, huh? They treated us and our wives like kings and queens for three days and three nights, giving us watches and everything. We had a ball. We even got a chance to work with kids, showing them a thing or two about ball. Granted, most of us were in our seventies and the physical prowess we once had was fading, but we still had the head knowledge needed to play baseball. After all, baseball involves more mental toughness than just about any sport out there.

In 2005, the Philadelphia Stars were honored with a sculpture and memorial park at Belmont and Parkside avenues, near where the Stars once played their home games. Bill is in the foreground with Mahlon Duckett (center) and Stanley Glenn (right). (Credit: Alejandro A. Alvarez, Philadelphia Daily News.)

And now let me say something about some of the movies on Negro League ballplayers. It's important that the legacy of the Negro League players be kept alive. Shoot, that's one reason why I wrote this book. But there's no need to lie about what happened.

That HBO movie *Soul of the Game*, which came out in 1996? One of the biggest lies I've ever seen. First off, you know that opening scene in the East-West game where Satchel is supposed to be pitching to Josh while Campy is catching? Impossible. Satchel played for the Kansas City Monarchs in the West, and Campy played for the Elite Giants in the East, so they couldn't have been teammates in an East-West game. Plus you remember that big scene in the kitchen when Jackie and Josh supposedly went at it because Josh was jealous of Jackie going to the majors? Never happened. Josh didn't even know Jackie personally.

At the end of that movie, there's some small print that says some of the scenes were made up for dramatic purposes. Well, no stuff! I don't know why they had to make up things to make the movie exciting. They did the same with *Bingo Long Travelling All-Stars and Motor Kings*. Nobody clowned and grinned as much as Bingo, not even the Indianapolis Clowns.

Just tell the truth about our leagues; that would be good enough. No dramatization is needed.

And we're far from being washed up. In fact, some of us and our wives were cast as extras in Oprah Winfrey's 1998 movie *Beloved*, based on the Pulitzer Prize-winning book by Toni Morrison. In the movie, Oprah plays Sethe, an escaped slave who kills her daughter and is haunted by her ghost. Danny Glover plays Sethe's lover, Paul D.

It seemed like a fluke how we got selected. We had a non-profit group called the Seven Philadelphia Stars that included me, Stanley Glenn, Larry Kimbrough, Wilmer Harris, Duckett, Benson, and Gould (who is a descendant of the founders of Gouldtown, New Jersey, which *Ebony* magazine called "American's Oldest Negro Community"). We were at Veterans Stadium for ceremonies marking the fiftieth anniversary celebration of Jackie Robinson. As we were coming off the field, a young lady named Kimberly came over and told Duckett she was going to call him about using us in the movie.

A few days later, they invited us to the movie set in Lancaster, Pennsylvania. They put us in a van and drove us to a beautiful hotel. We got there on a Sunday night and had a 5 a.m. Monday wake-up call. At 5:30 a.m., a van arrived at the hotel and took us to the set, where we got into our period costumes, you know, from the 1800s. But as soon as we finished dressing and came outside looking like small-town farmers, they threw dirt on us. We were baffled. We kept being told how expensive the costumes were and everything—but here they were dirtying up the clothes. Finally someone explained that the dirt cut the glare from the lights.

That Tuesday, we had a scene with Danny. He was coming out of a barbershop. Me, Duckett, Stanley, and Gould were sitting on the barbershop porch and were given our lines by director Jonathan Demme. We were supposed to be sitting around, shooting the breeze and gossiping about Oprah.

Well, we did eight takes of the scene. Eight! After our sixth try, Jonathan came over and said, "Boy, you guys are good." After our scene wrapped, Danny came over and sat on the stool, signing autographs and talking to everybody. Then my Sadie came over, and I introduced her to Danny. He looked up, grabbed her, and kissed her. Sadie said she was never going to wash her face again.

We returned two weeks later and were put up in a more elaborate hotel. And when we got to the set, we were surprised as heck. We each had our own trailers, with our names on the door. Talk about being big-time.

I enjoyed my movie experience. Everybody on the set was friendly. And I was amazed at what they could do. It didn't matter what time of night it was, those big lights could make it as bright as day. I mean, those people could even make it snow when it was hot and sunny outside. They brought in this big tank that blew "snow" all over the place. It didn't melt, but it was slippery.

I think Jonathan took a liking to me. I gave him one of our "Seven Philadelphia Stars" T-shirts. When he came to get me and Sadie to do a scene in the grocery store, I asked him if he got his gift. He pulled open his shirt, and sure enough, he was wearing the T-shirt.

I wish I could say that *Beloved* turned me into another Denzel Washington, but no such luck. The film opened in November 1998 to mixed reviews. Not nearly as many people went to see it as we had hoped. Maybe it was the subject—folks still have a hard time dealing with slavery in movies. And the story was hard to follow. To top it off, the barbershop scene with me and the fellows was left on the cutting room floor. I guess something had to go, because the movie was nearly three hours long.

Anyway, it's good we're getting some recognition, because many of us are dying off. Sadly, in April 1999, we lost Benson. He was eighty-five. The man was a fantastic ballplayer, and I respected him as our leader on and off the field. In fact, when he passed, he was first vice president of the Seven Philadelphia Stars Foundation Inc. that was started by the seven surviving Stars in the Philadelphia area. I will miss him. In January 2001, we lost Kimbrough. He was seventy-seven. Wilmer Harris passed in 2004. He was eighty. And on April 16, 2011, we lost my friend Stanley Glenn. He was eighty-four. So now we're down to three surviving Stars: me, Duckett, and Gould.

In June 2003, the great Larry Doby, the former Newark Eagle who broke the color barrier in the American League by playing for the Cleveland Indians—and the man involved in my controversial play at home plate in 1946—died in Montclair, New Jersey. He was seventy-nine. And in 2006, my buddy Buck O'Neil died in Kansas City, Missouri. He was ninety-four.

In 2002, Don Motley, who then was executive director of the Negro Leagues Baseball Museum, said there were about 250 Negro League players still alive. But the Negro League Baseball Players Association group, using a different time frame of play (1920–1950), put the number at fifty. Nowadays that number is bound to be smaller. And by either criterion, we Negro Leaguers are fading out.

And we are losing those black sportswriters responsible for chronicling the Negro Leagues. Sam Lacy of the Afro-American newspapers died in May 2003. He was ninety-nine years old and did much for us Negro players, especially Jackie. And Malcolm Poindexter, who wrote for the *Philadelphia Tribune* and became a groundbreaking broadcast journalist, died in March 2010. He was eighty-four.

Because of my age and health, I don't make public appearances or give public lectures like I use to. I loved speaking to people about the league. It's hard to believe that when I was still in school, I was as bashful as could be. I was good in math, algebra, and geometry, and I always knew the answer, but I wouldn't say anything. Those cute little white girls in class used to say, "Bill, you know the answer. Why don't you say it?" But for some reason, I was scared to put my hand up, you know. But when I became a leader in the Masons, I had no choice. I had to speak.

In 1992, Sadie was diagnosed with colon cancer. We went to doctors and prayed hard. I visited her in the hospital so often they joked about moving a bed in the room for me. Sadie survived, but soon she came down with Alzheimer's, just like my mother.

Bill and the love of his life, his wife Sadie, on the front porch of their house in West Philadelphia, July 1985. (Credit: Susan Winters, Philadelphia Daily News.)

I had problems too. I had a hernia operation. When Sadie went through her ordeal with colon cancer, I suffered a minor heart attack shoveling snow out of our driveway. So while Sadie was recuperating in one part of the hospital, I was recuperating on the hospital's second floor.

Then it was my prostate. The doctor found cancer cells in my prostate and wanted to operate, but I wasn't having none of that. I started taking herbs, and things improved—for a while. The doctors are watching it very closely.

My age and related health issues have taken their toll on these old baseball bones of mine. And then there is that big hole in my heart created eight years ago.

On October 23, 2003, the Lord called my sweet Sadie home. Sixty-three years we were married. Sixty-three wonderful years. Three wonderful children. Memories made great by our love for God and each other.

She was the prettiest woman I've ever seen, you hear me?

Ever.

CHAPTER 13

EPILOGUE

✲ ✲ ✲

I've been enshrined in three halls of fame, the Bob Douglas Hall of Fame in Ashland, Kentucky, the John Hunter Hall of Fame in New York City, and the Delaware County Black Baseball Hall of Fame in Chester, Pennsylvania. And I know what you're thinking. What about the big one, what about Cooperstown? That's a far ways off to me, and I'm not holding my breath. Shoot, I'm ninety-one. And truth be told, it's not important to me. What is important is that people know about the Negro Leagues and its players. We are important and living history.

Here are a few final words I want to pass on to you and your kids:

- Have a goal; go after what your heart wants the most.
- Keep God first, but don't let anybody stand in your way.
- Don't ever give up.
- When you're right, don't back down.
- Know your job better than the next guy.

And always be "Ready" to play.

On September 12, 2011, three months before his auto-biography was published, Bill died from pneumonia in Roxborough Hospital in Philadelphia. He was ninety-two.

ABOUT THE AUTHORS

* * *

William Walker "Ready" Cash, born February 21, 1919, was a catcher for the Philadelphia Stars of the Negro Leagues from 1943 to 1950. He was named to the prestigious East-West All-Star Team in 1948 and 1949, and in 1946, he was selected to play with the Satchel Paige All-Stars, but a broken thumb forced him to bow out of the game. Bill's stellar career also included stints in Cuba, Mexico, the Dominican Republic, Canada, and Venezuela. Enshrined in three local halls of fame, Bill earned his nickname "Ready" as a youngster because he was always ready to play ball. Bill is a thirty-third-degree Prince Hall Mason and was married to his late wife, Sadie, for sixty-three years.

Al Hunter Jr. spent twenty-eight years in the newspaper business - the last 17 with the *Philadelphia Daily News* - as an award-winning reporter and jazz columnist, editor, and editorial writer. He was editorial consultant for music legend Dionne Warwick's autobiography, *My Life, As I See It*, written with David Freeman Wooley. Al resides in Philadelphia, Pennsylvania, and is a former president of the Philadelphia Association of Black Journalists.

Made in the USA
Charleston, SC
05 July 2012